Praise for *Hip Mama* magazine

"*Hip Mama* is considered one of the best zines out there."

—*San Francisco Chronicle*

"Fun and irreverent."

—*USA Today*

"No sanctified endorsements of the usual myths about motherhood here. No neat checklists of all-too-easy parenting solutions or slick write-ups of professional experts telling how it's supposed to be done. . . . *Hip Mama* explores the real stuff of parenting with a proper recognition of the ambiguity of it all—and plenty of love and humanity."

—*Utne*

"It's the quality of the writing that sets *Hip Mama* apart."

—*The New Yorker*

"Childrearing gets cutting-edge treatment."

—*Chicago Tribune*

"Delightful."

—*Glamour*

"Ariel Gore is one of the world's frankest, funniest, and most incisive writers about motherhood."

—*San Francisco Metropolitan*

"The original punk rock parenting zine."

—*Punk Planet*

"America really does have something going for it."

—*Irish Times*

"*Hip Mama* is a startling good magazine. You and your mothers are to be congratulated."

—Miriam Patchen, Palo Alto, California

"*Hip Mama* sat on this crowded, oppressive desk for several days before I opened it—wrong move! It was an instant lift for what ails me, and I was thrilled once more by the wit, anger, rage, and sheer goodness of your staff and readers."

—Mary Kay Blakely, New York, New York

"Just when I was thinking that all the parenting mags were slick, commercial-filled tributes to the upwardly mobile and more-stuff-less-time lifestyle, *Hip Mama* is quietly glowing on the shelf at my local market. What a find you are—like biting into produce from our garden, still warm from the sun. . . ."

—Deb Michaels, Eugene, Oregon

"We are so excited to see a zine for moms who are above and beyond the mainstream, and who don't conform to the stereotypes of motherhood. Thanks for being here, and keep up the great work!"

—Kim Davenport, Portland, Oregon

"I enjoyed, savored, and was moved by every page."

—Fatimah Araneta, Valle de Bravo, Mexico

"You rule. *Hip Mama* has made a huge impact on my life for years. I stand proud to be a hip mama!"

—Meg, San Antonio, Texas

the
essential

Hip Mama

Writing from the
Cutting Edge of Parenting

edited by Ariel Gore

SEAL PRESS

Library of Congress Cataloging-in-Publication Data
Essential Hip mama : writing from the cutting edge of parenting /
[edited] by Ariel Gore.
    p. cm.
Anthology of articles published in the zine Hip Mama.
  ISBN 1-58005-123-5 (pbk.)
1. Mothers–United States. 2. Motherhood–United States. 3.
Parenting–United States. I. Gore, Ariel, 1970- II. Hip mama.

HQ759.E868 2004
306.874'3–dc22

                            2004019776

9 8 7 6 5 4 3 2 1

Cover design by Patrick David Barber
Interior design by Justin Marler
Printed in the United States of America by Worzalla
Distributed by Publishers Group West

Contents

Portrait of the Artist as a Young Mom

Transitions

Looking for Love

The Parental Is Political

Faith and Irreverence: UnVirgin Births

Lineage

Introduction

Ariel Gore

*I*n the fall of my senior year of college, I had a problem.

I'd been working insanely—baby on my back or crawling through the aisles of my lecture hall classes—for four years. I'd completed nearly all of my college credits, kept my growing daughter fed, made the honor roll, helped organize student moms to demand affordable daycare and a safe playground on campus, and managed to survive on an average of three and a half hours' sleep a night. But one assignment stood between my high school–dropout self and college graduation . . . a senior project.

I listened to my classmates describe plans for complex theses on communication theory and documentary films about race and class in America. Folks were heading off to New York to do research internships and planning for endless hours in the library. All I could think was: *Where am I gonna get a babysitter for this one?* I'd mastered the art of all-night essay writing and studying after my toddler had fallen asleep, but this grand finale assignment was no 10-page sociology paper or statistics test cramming session. I was completely freaked out. So I did what I'd always done when I couldn't wrap my mind around something: I tried to forget about it.

As my classmates' plans for earth-shattering investigations into media distortions became more and more involved, I hid behind the latest issues of *Ms.*, *Parenting*, *Bust*, and the *Utne Reader*, concocting schemes to land a job or make a living as a freelance journalist when I got out of school. Whenever my postgraduation thoughts morphed into thoughts of *if* I got out of school, I put the magazines down and focused my energy on cleaning up finger-painting mishaps or making spaghetti for the throngs of disheveled children who ran through our family student-housing complex.

And, as always, I drank coffee. I drank *a lot* of coffee.

My best friend and radical mama ally, Julie Bowles, was studying psychology at the time, and together we lamented the removal of "caffeine-induced organic mental disorder" from the American Psychiatric Association's list of official insanities. We were both obviously suffering from the disorder, and now we'd never be able to get insurance to cover it—even if we ever *did* manage to graduate and find jobs with psychiatric benefits.

Anyway, I must have been having one of my caffeine-induced organic episodes the night Julie made dinner for us all, and her youngest had thrown half of it across the living room floor. The older preschoolers played outside in a sprinkler, muddying up their freshly laundered clothes, while Julie's partner quietly recycled all the stupid parenting magazines they'd gotten free from their pediatrician. Julie was doing the dishes and I was boiling water for more coffee when she turned to me and asked, casually, what I'd come up with for my senior project. My proposal was due in the morning, wasn't it?

I laughed uneasily, surveyed the chaos around us, and joked, "I'm gonna make a *real* parenting magazine—the kids are gonna be a mess, half the moms are gonna be single, and no 'experts.' All the writers are gonna be in the trenches. In my zine, mamas will tell the *truth* about this shit. You'll be able to hear the baby screaming right through the middle of it."

Julie's partner cackled. He said, "What's it gonna be called? *Espresso Is My Co-Pilot?*"

"No, man. I'm gonna call it *Hip Mama.*"

Julie placed a mug in the dish rack, looked me up and down, and couldn't help but laugh: my ripped jeans, my stained T-shirt, my messed-up whitey-afro. Not exactly the picture of an early '90s hipster.

Just then my daughter hit her son over the head with the hose—or somebody hit somebody—and all hell broke loose outside. Screaming, muddy, cold, drenched chaos.

I got up early the next morning, made myself a cup of coffee, typed up a proposal for my half-baked idea for a *real* parenting zine, threw on a clean T-shirt but didn't bother to change out of the sweats I'd slept in, delivered my newly potty-trained daughter to preschool, stopped at the college café for a quick double shot of espresso, and headed across the green-grass campus to my communications senior seminar, hoping I'd be able to present my project plan with a straight face.

Sitting under the fluorescent lights, reading over my notes for *Hip Mama*, listening to the other proposals in which my classmates described their plans to deconstruct 200 years of feminist theory or prove that the advertising industry was directly responsible for alcoholism in low-income communities and potentially legally liable for it, I felt like such a dork. I was planning to collect a bunch of articles with titles like "Barbie's Liberation" and "The Chaos Theory of Parenting" and "Mothers Don't Fart." My professors and peers had put up with me nursing my daughter through lectures when I couldn't find childcare, turning in papers with scribbles in the margins, and habitually slipping into baby talk when discussing economic theory or media monopolies. Surely *this* would be the limit. I wracked my brain for a spur-of-the-moment substitute idea. Something that would prove I'd really been digesting all that information from my textbooks, teachers, research projects, and class discussions. Something *serious.* I drew a blank. *Four years of higher education and what was I qualified to dissect?* My classmates had phrases like "postmodern media globalization" and "paradigm shifting." *What did I have? Postmodern diapering?* But it was my turn, so I stood up, and tried not to make eye contact with anyone as I began. *What was I going to say, anyway?* I opened my mouth and, miraculously, a quote right out of one of those boring communications textbooks fell from my lips: "It was the legendary press critic A. J. Liebling who said, 'Freedom of the press is guaranteed only to those who own one.'"

That last double shot of espresso did not fail me, and I rolled through my academic-sounding preamble before laying it out for everyone: In *Hip Mama,* parenting would get cutting-edge treatment.

The weird thing was, when I put it that way, it didn't sound like a joke anymore. I'd deconstruct Disney, expose the infant-formula marketing industry, speak the truth about the fact that I hadn't had a good night's sleep in years. I'd heard parenting belittled in theory discussions and the media alike. Maybe I'd felt like a dork only because I'd believed all the people who scoffed at motherhood. But now, I explained, I would exercise my right to freedom of the press: I'd own one.

"Desktop publishing," my cowboy hat–wearing professor nodded.

"Actually, I don't have a desk,' I admitted. I'd somehow managed to get through nearly four years of school without even owning a computer. "Kitchen counter publishing."

A smirk and a nod. Project proposal approved.

Clichéd but true: If, on my way to my next class that bright morning in late fall 10 years ago, anyone had stopped to warn me that I'd just signed up for a career that would last at least a decade, I'd have rolled my eyes: *Yeah, right.* That I would put together the first issue of *Hip Mama* for my senior project and then produce another and another. That the mainstream press would write stories about the zine. That I'd be invited to debate then–Speaker of the House Newt Gingrich on MTV. That I'd write parenting books and one day get calls from national TV talk show producers looking to me as the "expert" on everything from potty training to getting through school with a baby on your back. That Julie and I would host a "Hip Mama Hour" on Free Radio Berkeley. That the coffee-inspired zine would in turn inspire websites, community groups, and annual gatherings of radical moms. That I would one day get a call from a reporter at the *Los Angeles Times* asking me how it felt to have founded a "movement." That my little zine would be called groundbreaking, lifesaving, kick-ass awesome. I would have thought my fortune-teller was suffering from "caffeine-induced organic mental disorder" herself. But that's the way it happened. I never got a real job after college—or grad school. I made *Hip Mama* my job. Low pay. Long hours. No insurance. Still headquartered in my kitchen. But mine. It's a free press because I own it.

These days, I get at least one letter a day from some mama somewhere telling me that *Hip Mama* saved her sanity, changed her life, inspired her to get real and not check her personality at the door just because she was a mother now. But I could just as easily say that *Hip Mama* saved *my* sanity, changed *my* life. It earned me a college degree and inspired me to get and stay real. I don't know what it feels like to have founded a "movement" because I didn't. I founded a zine. And the parents who sent me their essays and their art and their exposés and their own chaos theories taught me that I wasn't alone even when the mainstream parenting mags made me feel freakish and marginalized.

What was true when I was trying to come up with a senior project and what is true today: Motherhood has been my defining life experience. It is no small thing. When I started to write about that experience 10 years ago, the only other writers I read who admitted to sharing similar feelings seemed to be antifeminist "family values" wives who believed that women without children were somehow unfeminine, that a woman's worth could and should be measured by what she produced from her womb. The feminist writings I could find waxed philosophical about the institution of motherhood and explored real and deep truths about women's ambivalence, but too often harped on the oppression of it all rather than the powerful and shit-kicking good times. The magazine articles, when they weren't written by those so-called experts telling me what to do and when, described organic earth-mama perfection or Kodak moments in nuclear two-minivan families.

What I couldn't find back then were the voices of women like me and my radical mama allies—independent women who were raising their kids with love and fierceness, who could admit to their imperfections and fears, who cared to deconstruct Disney or who fell in love with Mister Rogers, whose feelings about motherhood ran from horror to joy on any given day, who could admit, as one writer did in issue 13 of *Hip Mama,*

I dearly love my children and do not wish them gone.
As a matter of fact, it is precisely the love I feel for

these people, a complex, many-faceted love unparalleled by any other I have known, that makes the condition of motherhood so unbearable. That I can never do right by them, that they can never live a pain-free existence, that I unthinkingly caused some of their pain, that the world I brought them into isn't good enough for them—all these are sources of anguish to me.

What I couldn't find were the voices of the mamas who worried about sexism in cartoons, who struggled to hang on to their own identities while allowing themselves to be defined by their roles as mothers, who appreciated the ambiguity of it all, who found themselves sometimes alienated from both the minivan set and the granola-eaters, and who, if given a platform, would be willing to tell their truths.

When I started *Hip Mama*, I had been a teen mom, a welfare mom, a single mom, a college mom. I was young, poor, urban. The plan from the start was that the zine would be reader-written, so I expected to receive essay submissions from other young and poor moms. I thought the zine would attract readers and writers like myself. But I discovered, almost immediately, that telling the truth about our experiences as mothers doesn't necessarily attract others like us—it attracts people who want to tell *their* truths about motherhood, no matter how different those experiences may be. The readers of *Hip Mama* are as diverse a group as the writers: There are teen moms and fiftysomething moms, single moms and married moms, straight moms and queer moms, college moms and rural moms, midwives and bank tellers.

The zine has always had a political bent, so let's face it: *Hip Mama* can only count a handful of Republicans among its loyal readers. Diversity does have its limitations. But for me, the parental and the political have always been inextricably entwined. There are morals and values espoused in every fairy tale. *Sesame Street* is a political television show. If the Speaker of the House wants to blame young mothers for the nation's economic problems, I consider it my duty to be willing to show up and make my humble attempt to take him to task for that. Whether or not the president decides to send 100,000 children to fight his next war matters to me as a mother. Child support, family leave acts, domestic violence initiatives, and public education funding are more than faraway bills in Congress. They affect our daily lives, the ways in which we can support our children. They are political issues, but they begin and end in our living rooms and nurseries.

Looking back through 10 years of *Hip Mama*, I realize that the zine has grown and changed in ways both predictable and unexpected. I was a 23-year-old college senior in Oakland, California, when I published the first issue. My daughter had just turned four. Now I'm a 33-year-old editor, writer, and teacher in Portland, Oregon. And my baby is a cheerleader. The zine has followed my interests as a mother and an editor. Stories on weaning abounded when I was trying to get my daughter off the tit. The question of public education versus homeschooling took center stage as I struggled to find the right place for Maia to start school. Essays on family court seemed most relevant during my seven-year odyssey as a perpetual litigant. And as Maia enters adolescence, I search for the voices of the soulful mothers of teenagers who have come before me.

When the journalists and producers call me as an "expert," I have to laugh. Whenever I've needed parenting advice, I've put out a call for submissions.

The contributors and readers of *Hip Mama* have taught me how to be a mother, not the other way around. From Julie, I learned to accept chaos and laugh through the insanity. From Opal Palmer Adisa, I learned what it means to be soulful and confident, and that attachment parenting is applicable even after we've sent the kids off to college. From Nina Hagen, I learned to stay faithful and not worry about being too freakin' weird. To try to list everyone and their contributions to my sanity as a mom would be to become super-dork—one of those people with a crumpled list at the Academy Awards, shouting random names long after the get-off-the-stage music has been cranked up.

My point is that *Hip Mama* has been as much of a lifesaver for me as it has been for anyone. Occasionally through the years, I've considered quitting. Ceasing publication and getting a real job. But if I stopped publishing *Hip Mama*, where would I read about Barbie's liberation and the ever-expanding chaos theory of parenting? Where would I read the truth about the defining experience of my life? As we learned in Communication 101, "Freedom of the press is guaranteed only to those who own one." And so I'll own my free press. And if I do my work well, so will you—groundbreaking, lifesaving, kick-ass awesome mamas, all.

In this book, you'll find some of the best articles and essays I've had the honor of publishing over the last decade in *Hip Mama*. These are the writings that have sustained me, educated me, and made me laugh. These are truths that have inspired me to be a better mother and soothed me even when I blew it bigtime. These are the big-hearted, crazy-brave voices I couldn't find 10 years ago, the ones I wasn't even sure existed that night at Julie's when I'd had too much coffee to drink and got a harebrained idea.

Nobody Said It Would Be Like This

Sunday	Monday	Tuesday	Wednesday
4 Landlord calls: "Just wondering if you have any intention of paying rent."	**5** Try to dye pink hair brown for family court. It turns green!	**6** Tell therapist about hair-dyeing fiasco. She sez: "I can hear that."	**7** Go with "natural black" dye. Kid sez: "Your hair's gonna fall out!"
11 Get 29 voice mails from ex, all saying: "Everyone knows yr crazy."	**12** Notice hair turning pink again.	**13** Take kids to exotic bird fair. Get turded on. Therapist sez: "I can hear that."	**14** Get accused of stalking ex. Get cleared when friend sez: "She never leaves home."
18 Six-year-old's tooth falls out. Do 17 loads laundry. Panic: She hid tooth in laundry!	**19** Get notice from DMV saying my right to operate a motor vehicle is history.	**20** Tell therapist life sucks & so does she. She sez: "I can hear that."	**21** Join Church of the Born Again Losers. Buy Rocket Espresso.
25 Take kids to various fathers for visits. Try to bleach hair. It turns orange.	**26** Sit in family court staring at clock. Calculate lawyer's fee at five cents/minute.	**27** Bring therapist Miracle-Ear as gift. She is not amused.	**28** Kid sez Easter Bunny, Santa, & God are all bogus. Rethink family values.

Thursday	Friday	Saturday
1 On way home from school, seven-year-old sez: "Mom, you are sooo retro!"	**2** Dye friend's hair kitchen-sink version of Exene Cervenka's. Do dishes.	**3** Take kids to various fathers for visits. Get fix-it ticket for busted tail-light.
8 Buy suit for family court. Attend voodoo invocation, then PTA meeting.	**9** Go to "friends & family day" at school to hear kids sing "Stand by Me."	**10** Secretly glad I never took last year's Xmas lights down—it's that time again.
15 Pre-press guy marvels at my productivity. Explain: "I never clean house."	**16** Dress for family court. Kid sez: "You look positively weird."	**17** Go see Ani DiFranco show. Notice my hair is starting to fall out.
22 Exene look-alike sez: "You must have done something bad in a past life."	**23** Ask kid what she wants for Xmas. She sez: "A flamingo & an elephant."	**24** Go to woods to offer ablutions to Our Lady of Class Struggle.
29 Braid hair & sit in back row of family court coaching mamas all day.	**30** Get henna tattoo. Looks like burn. Random people on street are concerned.	**31** Yell at tattoo artist, yell at DMV, fire therapist, hire cleaning lady.

yo mama's daybook

This Is Your Life

Fern Capella

his is your life when you're in a dream at 5 A.M., running fast with your arms empty, and you wake up to a screech and you think maybe you hopped a train, but then you feel something warm next to you in bed, and you remember

you had a baby three weeks ago.

And he's crying, so you reach over to soothe your precious baby and pull him up on top of you and as you do his diaper comes off and his poop is now all over you, so you summon the courage to stand up and clean up, so now you're naked as your parents walk through your room smiling, "Good morning," on their way to get coffee 'cause

you're 21 and single

and you're living in their living room. But not for long 'cause their next question is, "When do you think you'll be up to moving out?" and you think, "When do I think I'll be up to moving my body?" but you smile bravely and say, "Probably by next week." So they leave so you can breathe, but breathing is for the baby who you remember again and check on 'cause

breath is such a fragile thing.

Then your stitches tug and you can't imagine any of this ending, but then you can't imagine any other beginning than the one of this amazing life you call your son, and the stupid "You Are My Sunshine" song that set you hysterically crying in front of your baby's pediatrician yesterday as you thought of the second part—when the sunshine is taken away—and you think, "How could I take *that?*" and you fully realize a mother's terror.

Those poor mothers everywhere.

But really you could sob all day, and who has time 'cause you're a mother now and your three-ton tits are the last place you have been attacked in this war against your body as you hold one in each hand to shower while you have head out/ass in to sing your baby ga-ga songs about maybe getting a fucking break from someone sometime.

Like his father, that slime.

And your mother hears you and is appalled and you are disgusted with yourself and swear his name will never be mentioned when your baby knows what you're saying even though it seems like he always has with the beautiful way he surveys you and your heart hits the floor.

You love him like sapphires under your tongue.

And who else but his father calls to say he remembers why he made your baby and he could love you if you let him make another one. And you think that even you didn't have anything to do but host the miracle that was being formed inside you and this asshole getting some ass one night most certainly did not either, so you thank him for his microscopic gift of one in ten billion sperm that happened to make the prettiest baby you've ever seen and hang up thinking,

It's mostly between you and God now.

And so you pull some energy out from somewhere deep 'cause you realize you won't be wanting any breaks from Him, and you get you and your baby dressed and make your way to the store and there, in the midst of checkout, you're roused from this seemingly endless daze to find the store clerk holding your whining baby with spit-up on his dark blue uniform and you writing a bad check with shaky fingers and the lady behind you in line dying to find out why your skin is whiter than white, like Tide with Bleach, and your baby looks like a Cuban who has just been rescued from the seas, and you snarl and say, "You wanna see my stretch marks?" 'cause

he could only be your baby.

You get nauseous to think otherwise, though that seems to be a better option as your mother mentions later that, "It's never too late to consider adoption," and you tell her, "It's never too late to consider suicide," and it's all just so sugar sweet. If you could just melt for a moment with your baby and rest, you might just see clear but you're interrupted in your merging by a phone call from your very childless, gay best friend who wants to go out later with you and "it"—the baby—but he's nervous that everyone might think he's the father 'cause the poor kid doesn't have one and

that's the curse of the single mother.

You're always left open for insult and somehow you're always tough enough to take it and

that's the blessing of the single mother.

It's not til much later that you have time to write these things and your back is tired and your bones are tired and even your pen seems tired, but the paper is your lover and you tell it everything and you tell it how you're terrified and how you're probably a terrible mother but only on the shitty days and you tell it how you've never imagined a love so consuming and close to God as you have for this tender life sleeping in a curl next to you and you doze off exhausted to wake an hour later, around 5 A.M.

to a screech.

"You're the Stupidest Mommy in the World, and I Hate You!"

Christine Malcolm

A few months ago when my middle son, Finn, was beginning to come into his own with the English language, I was treated to the words every mother knows are coming some day: "I hate you, mommy!" Actually, my gentle two-year-old's exact words were: "You're the stupidest mommy in the world, AND I hate you!"

For this my yoni has been stretched to the size of the Carlsbad Caverns. For this my belly, once flat and strong, falls next to me when I lie down, reminiscent of the skin around a Saint Bernard's mouth. For this my breasts, after ballooning with milk and hormones, are now wrinkled and withered, sagging like two cold griddle cakes pasted to my chestal area. I have to wear a bra if I want to hoist them up to the proper breast locale. And I hate bras.

For this I now live in fear of becoming an invisible, sexless drone who thinks of nothing but parent council meetings and MusicGarten classes. Worst of all, for this I am forced to expose myself to the other mothers I encounter in the morning drop-off at school and childcare as the slovenly, tardy, wacko parent I am.

I am a woman who spent many younger years living in a van with friends and lovers, following rock bands and camping in cities and wildernesses across America. I imagine these other mothers as women who joined sororities in college and went sailing in Quogue and the Vineyard during breaks. They now drive super-SUVs, like Range Rovers and Land Cruisers. Call me bitter, but I am disgusted by anyone who lacks the insight to recognize the greed and insecurity that motivates one to own a car that costs more than most American families' combined annual salaries, to speak nothing of the environmental effect of SUVs. Yeah, maybe I'm bitter, but it strikes me as a bit thoughtless, is all.

The *New York Times Magazine* recently ran an article on "Mean Girls," an apparently news-breaking piece on how cruel and duplicitous adolescent girls are to each other. I especially loved one anecdote about a 13-year-old girl who would preface all her scathing comments with "No offense, but . . ." As in, "No offense, but your hair looks like it hasn't been washed in a month and your kid is dressed like the white trash I'm sure you must be. . . ."

Okay, maybe I'm a teensy bit bitter about these other super-SUV mommies. "No offense, but your competitive, materialistic, clonelike excuse for a life makes me want to puke." *No offense.*

I have three kids. All boys. The eldest is eight, the second is three, and the baby is now a year. While I was pregnant with my first son, Bo, I had many firmly held convictions about child rearing. I believed my child would, by osmosis, hate television and junk food. I imagined him as an outgoing, long-ringlet-haired, inquisitive angel, cutely dancing barefoot next to his dad, Bruce, and me at folk festivals and begging for frozen rice-milk pops and falafel. My gypsy years had led me to believe that having kids was a simple matter—you just pop them in the backpack and they became radically cool human beings because you, of course, are a radically cool human being. You expose them to the "right" things, environments, and people, and they grow up to be fascinating, well-balanced adults with good politics and healthy teeth.

Then, on a fateful Tuesday morning in January, I gave birth to Bowen. Bo, my first lumpkin boy, nine and a half pounds of plump-assed love. My deepest joy. My most stirring passion. The child who has given me the clearest lesson that parents are merely the cab drivers, not the tour guides. The little buggers are sent to you by the forces that be, and your job is to transport them to their chosen destination safely, not to direct their trip. Anyone who says, "It's how you raise 'em," either hasn't had kids or was drinking heavily during his or her children's formative years.

Bowen shattered my fantasies of motherhood as quickly as you can say "Pokémon." As a baby, he was blissfully unattached to all of my preconceived notions about who I would shape him to be. He didn't realize I believed I would lead all my children to be friendly, flexible, and secure. So he glared at strangers in the supermarket who stopped to coo at him, snarling, "Don't look at me." Tantruming, he refused to do any kind of stint in childcare. In fact, he refused almost all babysitters, except our friend Gina, who was the consummate Italian mama. She showered him with so much love, even his trepid heart couldn't refuse her.

As he grew older, he became known as the "easy" toddler because he would watch videos for hours on end. I could bring him to the Planned Parenthood clinic where I work as a midwife, and he would sit in the staff kitchen watching TV for an entire day, eating Goldfish crackers, not making so much as a peep. Are you impressed by my wonderful mothering style yet? There were many years of guilt and doubt. Was my work outside the home fucking my kid up? Why was he so ornery? And why, oh why, did he like Barney?

All this is to say, I guess, that Bo has brought me on my knees to the truth: He is a gorgeous little person who is nothing like the child inhabiting my pre-parent fantasies. And in turn, I am not the Zen, self-less, creative, blissed-out mom I had imagined I would be. Bo is shy, sweet, moody, and internal. He loves TV and Game Boy. In fact, he is respected in his class as something of a guru of Game Boy. Oh, the things to make a mother proud.

I am demanding, cranky, self-absorbed, and conflicted. I am often more concerned about what I am going to do with my life than what happened at school today. I am sometimes a raving bitch. I am sometimes a fun, freewheelin' mama. You never know.

All of this is the truth. The most amazing truth is that the reality of who we are, *Rugrats* tapes and all, is much more precious to me than any rigid idea I may have held before. When my stinky-breathed, bony-legged, computer game–diggin' little boy climbs into my bed and snuggles next to me in the morning, every damn thing in the world is right.

Which brings me to another Hallmark mothering moment. While lying in bed all together one morning, Bo looked at my body and laughed, "Ladies have REALLY fat butts!" *No offense, but . . .*

I looked down at my hips, spread across the mattress like rolled-out stollen dough. He was right. This lady has a fat butt. Shane was climbing on my belly with an amorous look and Finn was edging to get as close to me as possible without actually pushing his baby brother down, which would get him into trouble. Both were oblivious to my laughable bodily condition. Only Bo was old enough to understand that by some standards my tush was something to be viewed with humor or distaste. For this I had children?

Bruce said to me, "Hey, J.Lo has a HUGE can!" Not quite the response I was going for. Even on my best day, 15 years ago, my ass wasn't at all like J.Lo's. Her huge can and mine are of different species. No, the response I would like is something like this: "Your stretched-out, flubbery body is amazing. It bears the record of the work you have done as a mother, the love you have let pass through you. It is real. It is sexy. It is the most beautiful thing I, as your partner, could ever wish for. And furthermore, the cultural warping of women's body images is a sick and evil marketing technique perpetrated on us by misogynist, life-sucking advertisers and media."

I actually think Bruce believes these things, but he just doesn't say them. Maybe I kid myself. I flirted dangerously with a serious eating disorder when I was younger and honey, I tell you, I ain't goin' back. I am determined to be generous to my flubbery self, fat butt and all. I am determined to teach my kids that beautiful bodies come in all shapes, sizes, and tones. I am determined to be grateful for this old gal I was given to walk around in, complete with cellulite and an incomprehensible amount of excess body hair.

When I see the half-starved, spinning class–chiseled SUV moms at the community pool, sporting their stylish tankinis, I will remember it is revolutionary in this society for a woman to appreciate her own, unique body just the way it is. Revolutionary. I mean it. That powerful. That important. And on a bad day, if all else fails, I will whisper to my like-spirited, slack-bellied mom friend, "No offense, but don't you think those bottoms make her butt look fat?"

News Flash

This Is Your Brain, This Is Your Brain Without Gravity

Raising kids in outer space could be a lot trickier than you imagined. Scientists revealed studies in October suggesting that children born in space might suffer permanent nervous system damage unless exposed to Earthlike gravity at key points during their development. It seems that the youngsters' neurons would be permanently wired for the low-gravity world of space and they would have trouble walking on Earth unless they were periodically spun around in centrifuges to make sure they received their proper dose of Gs.

Mothers Don't Fart

Laura Allen Sandage

"Who did it?"

"Not me."

"Me, neither. Cross my heart."

"C'mon, who cut the cheese?"

The Babysitting Kids, as we called them, were all standing around the kitchen sink while my mother cleaned up after snack. They were a varied, ever-changing group with whom we shared our early mornings and late afternoons during the years Mama had a daycare license.

"All right," Mama finally admitted. "I did it."

Shocked giggles.

The youngest at the time, little Kristin, was one of those very serious six-year-olds, with dark bangs cut precision-straight across a pale forehead.

"But . . ." Kristin blinked. "Mothers don't fart!"

"Of course they do. All mothers fart." In three words, my mother dragged all the mothers of the world down with her.

Then ensued a flurry of curious probes from the older kids. Do grandmothers fart, too? How do you know that all mothers fart? How about teachers? Do policemen fart?

Mama knew how to put an end to these questions. Slowly and deliberately she informed them: "Even the president of the United States farts."

Stunned silence. Maybe a gasp or two. This was during the Ford administration, when the White House never would have released such information.

Eventually, the Babysitting Kids filed out of the kitchen into the backyard, John and Arnett soberly discussing presidential flatulence, Tammi giggling, and Kristin still too stunned to speak. Perhaps in those few moments, their view of authority figures had been altered irrevocably. I like to think Mama's quiet brand of insurrection could seep into young minds just as surely as her silent-but-deadly farts could sink into our cheap upholstered furniture.

The Ideal Candidate to Raise My Child

Ingrid Block

As a young girl, my aspirations were not aimed in the same direction as those of the other girls on my block. They watched their parents and learned to imitate the appropriate roles (mother, wife). I contemplated the bleak prospect of growing up to be like the women in my family whose roles were limited to domestic servitude and domestic prostitution to an indifferent patriarchy: cooking, cleaning, expecting a baby every few years. This spelled death for my ambitious mind. I knew that my life would be different. I presumed that this meant I did not want to be a mother.

I thought about all of this when I found myself unexpectedly pregnant at 25 years old. But I was not prepared for the intense emotions that would overcome me as I tried to decide what to do. No matter what I would eventually decide, I knew that my life would be forever changed.

In an attempt to be fair to myself (and to my unborn child), and to explore all of my options, I paid a visit to some local law offices that specialized in adoption. I met with a female lawyer in one of the firms and clearly explained that the purpose of my visit was to gather information. She seemed more than happy to oblige. In order to be considered for this particular firm's "open adoption" plan, she explained, I would have to turn over my prenatal medical records. This seemed like a reasonable request, and I cooperated, divulging my doctor's name and my medical record number.

Two days after the initial visit, I received an urgent phone call from the lawyer. She wanted to meet with me immediately. When I arrived, there was a young couple sitting in her office. "This couple would like to adopt your baby, Ingrid. . . ."

I was stunned. The couple stared at me with pity, and the lawyer handed me a document to "look over," explaining all the while what a great set of parents couple X would make, mostly because of their "financial stability," church attendance, and lovely tract home in San Whatever.

As for me, the lawyer looked at the couple and explained, "Ingrid is a student, she's not quite finished with school yet, and this is what she needs to do." All three nodded in agreement. I stared out the window, my mind racing. I was much too confused and sad to read or comprehend the papers that had been drawn up in anticipation of my vulnerability. I felt a surge of humiliation. Tears welled up in my eyes. I excused myself and left.

This meeting was followed by almost daily (uninvited) phone calls from the attorney, and even calls to my doctors from someone wanting to check on "the status of the fetus."

How could I rationalize handing over my baby just because of discrepancies in my bank account? Did having good credit make someone a good parent?

All of this put my thoughts on my pending motherhood into perspective. I am a lot more than a woman in her 20s who "needs to finish school." I have survived an abusive, neglectful childhood to become a productive and well-adjusted adult. I have worked in the music industry, started my own business, made a movie, traveled the world independently, studied languages and culture. I know right from wrong. And I decided that being a mother didn't necessarily mean being a servant; that I didn't have to live the thankless life that so many women, like those in my family, had.

When I thought about the qualities I wanted in the parents who would raise my child, I realized I wanted someone with the life experience I had earned. I wanted someone with dirt under her fingernails. I wanted someone who was focused, who had morals, integrity, and an openness to growth.

And I realized that I already knew the ideal candidate.

News Flash

Get a Grip, Mama

A woman in the Eureka, California, area has reportedly been grabbing babies from total strangers and breastfeeding them, according to local police.

"Every child needs lactate nourishment," the woman told a shocked mother during the last incident. Patrol Sergeant Len Johnson said that so far no infants have been harmed, but authorities are worried the situation could "escalate."

The Baby Bank

Kathy Briccetti

How old is your son?"

"He's three and a half," I say to the woman sitting next to me on the bench at Totland Park. Then I brace myself for what comes next. It always does.

"Wow! He's big!" she says, looking at my son climbing the slide and then back at me. "Is your husband tall?"

"Well," I start. My heart is pounding and my brain is racing because I'm trying to decide if I feel safe getting into this discussion with her. I'm wondering whether I have enough energy at the moment to carry it out. But I continue, too quickly. My words run together because I'm nervous about how she'll react.

"I don't have a husband, my partner is a woman, and we used a donor from the sperm bank to get pregnant."

Then I'm done. It's out and I look up at her and wait for her response. There is a five-beat pause followed by a long "Oh . . ." and then, "Wow!"

There's another silence, which I quickly fill. "Yeah, we don't know who the donor is, but we know a lot about him. We have a really thick

21

file with medical and personal and family information. And we used the same donor for both of our kids." As I say this I gesture toward my other son toddling by. "The donor is a big guy."

"Wow," she says again. "Have you seen a picture of him? What does he look like?"

"No. We didn't get to see a picture. All we have is a description of him. He's six feet, and he has green eyes and straight, light brown hair. And I know how tall his parents and grandparents and sisters and brother are and we have all their medical histories."

As I tell her this, I think again how odd it is to know all these facts but still not really know what the donor looks like. I often wonder about the shape of his nose, chin, and eyes. Does my son look more like him or me? If I saw the donor on the street somewhere, would I instantly feel a jolt of recognition? *Those are Evan's eyes!* Or does Evan have a blending of our features so that he doesn't look like the donor at all?

"Yeah, I wish I could see him," I tell her. "Maybe someday I will."

"What do you mean?" She gets up from the bench to push her daughter on the swing. I follow her, keeping an eye on my children now playing together in the sand.

"We used the sperm bank in Oakland because they have this identity release program. Some of the donors have agreed to release their names when the kids turn 18. So if my kids want to learn more about the donor or even contact him later, they can. That was important to my partner and me. My father was adopted so I know how it feels to know nothing about half of my ancestry."

"That's amazing," she says. She is picking up sand toys and getting ready to leave. It's lunchtime. Evan calls for me, crying because his little brother has just pounded him on the head with a shovel. My adult conversation is over for today. And as usual I have only told part of our story.

When my partner Pam and I first talked about having children, we hadn't known anyone who had used a sperm bank. We considered asking someone we knew to be the donor, or using a go-between to find someone, but those options made us nervous. Picturing a donor someday taking us to court for custody convinced us that the sperm bank was the best method for us. If I'd had more time I could have told the woman in the park how I got pregnant. How for months every morning before prying open an eyelid I reached for the thermometer on the nightstand and slipped it under my tongue, trying not to fall back to sleep, afraid I'd bite off the end of the thermometer, spilling mercury and glass shards into my mouth. Then writing down the temperature to a tenth of a degree and plotting it each day on my graph, waiting for the telltale dip of two-tenths of a degree that meant I'd ovulate within the next 24 hours. If I had put my monthly graphs together side by side in a line they would have looked like the readings on a heart monitor machine, up, down, up, down, *blip, blip.*

I learned how to check my cervical mucus and use an ovulation predictor kit from the drugstore so by the time I was ready to inseminate, I couldn't see how it would take more than one try.

I would have told that other mother about the day Pam and I went to the sperm bank to pick out donors. How we sat together on a gray-white vinyl love seat in a tiny consultation room and read through a stack of thick file folders.

"Okay, how do you want to do this?" I asked.

"Well, we have one hour paid for so let's do a quick run-through and toss out the ones that we talked about—no breast cancer, no asthma, no 20/200 vision. Nothing that runs in your family, right?" She handed half of the stack to me and opened up the top folder.

"Oh, wow. This guy weighs 250 pounds and he's five-eleven. I wonder what he looks like."

"He could be a body builder." I lowered my voice. "Or do you think they use fat guys as donors?" For an instant I looked around for a hole in the wall that might be hiding a camera. Or a little sliding window, with tiny double doors, like the kind you slip your urine sample through at the doctor's office. I pictured the office staff listening in and getting a good laugh.

We read quietly for awhile, tossing charts into a pile between us.

"Mother had breast cancer."

"Only a high school education. I'd rather go with number 17, the PhD."

"Lemme see that. Pam, he's only 18, for Christ's sake! How could he have any more education?"

"An 18-year-old, do you believe that? Would you want our kid to be fathered by an 18-year-old? This is unreal!" We laughed. Nervous, exasperated laughs.

When we brought our six-pack cooler with the sun-faded red lid home from the sperm bank the first time, we didn't dare open it for fear the dry ice would disappear. We didn't know how many days we'd have to wait for that dip in morning temperature. When the time finally came and we opened the cooler for the first time, we must have looked like a couple of kids waiting for the jack-in-the-box to jump out and surprise us. Then, with her hand in a grass-stained gardening glove, Pam reached under the dry ice, now letting off its misty vapor into the room.

As I waited I swung my legs back and forth from my perch at the end of the bed. I was dressed in my "thirtysomething" nightshirt and my red-checked flannel robe because it was time to go to bed. Although it was the middle of summer, I felt cold. My body shivered slightly, like it did when I had to give a presentation at work. *This is so weird. What am I about to put into my body?*

I knew that the donors were tested for all sorts of diseases, including HIV, and that semen was quarantined for six months until the donor returned for more blood tests. Still, I wondered if this stuff would hurt me somehow. And what would come out in 40 weeks? A little alien? What if there was a horrible disease that ran in the donor's family and he forgot to mention it during the medical history?

Suddenly Pam said, "I can't find it!"

Oh, God, I thought, they forgot to put it in the cooler. We'll have to drive all the way back to the sperm bank. The clock is ticking. That egg could be popping out right now and we'll miss our chance this month. But before I could go any further Pam pulled out a zip-top sandwich bag packed with more dry ice. Inside the bag was a tiny vial, the size of a perfume sample from a department store. It was frosty on the outside, and inside we could see a dropperful of frozen white liquid; it filled the container halfway. On the outside the number 23 and a date from almost a year before were written in fine-tip black permanent marker. We both laughed.

Pam put the vial under her arm like a mother duck keeping her egg warm. I giggled. "Well, that ought to do the trick," I told her. But I felt more fear settling into my gut. How will people treat us, I wondered. How will they treat our children? Will our children suffer because of how we are creating them? Am I being selfish because I want to be pregnant, to give birth, and to raise my babies?

As I held the vial, Pam pulled off the tiny cap and gently put the end of the syringe, blunt without a needle, on the bottom of the vial. "Careful," I said. "You don't want to kill any of them getting in there." Pam pulled back the plunger in slow motion, as if she were working in a laboratory with volatile substances. When all of the liquid had been withdrawn, the syringe stuck to the bottom of the vial briefly and made a soft suction noise.

"Okay, I got it. Are you ready?"

"Um hmm." I lay back on the bed with my hips propped up on several pillows and lifted my nightshirt to my waist.

"Is that the right place? Does that hurt?" Gingerly, Pam placed the syringe and slowly pushed the plunger. She tossed the syringe and its wrapper into the wastebasket and lay down next to me. She nuzzled her head until it rested on my shoulder. "We did it." She smiled. I looked at her and smiled. "Yeah, we did."

Slowly we moved from cuddling to caressing to making love. We fell asleep joined like spoons, our favorite position.

After the first try, since we had done everything by the book, I assumed I was pregnant. Pam bought a home pregnancy test, and I planned to call my new obstetrician for my first prenatal appointment. On the earliest day that my pregnancy could be confirmed with the home test, Pam and I laughed as we sat on the edge of the bathtub, tore open the box, and agreed when we would announce our news. So when the blue line on the tester did not appear, I was shocked. I repeated the pregnancy test the next day and got the same result. My disbelief turned to disappointment, but in two weeks I was eager to try again. We repeated the process over two more months and by the third insemination I dreaded the two-week wait. What was wrong? Maybe I hadn't ovulated or maybe the semen sample was flawed. *(Maybe they put something else in that vial we paid a hundred bucks for!)* Maybe the timing wasn't exactly right after all, or maybe at 35 I was too old. Pam tried to cheer me up, but I could hear her own disappointment in her voice.

Pam didn't join me in the bathroom for the third pregnancy test. I waited by myself, then glanced down at the tester before I tossed it in the trash. But this time there was an extra blue line. It took only an instant to realize what it meant and my feelings flip-flopped. All by myself in the bathroom I shouted, "Yes!" Our scientific method had worked. We had done it.

Pam and I had decided to be honest about our conception method to everyone. We did not want to keep secrets from our children or force them to keep secrets. Now we want them to know the truth about how they came to be, and that we are not ashamed but proud of how we made them. It hasn't been as difficult as I thought it would be, probably because there are so many two-mom families around here, and there seems to be a growing tolerance—at least in the San Francisco Bay Area.

During my first pregnancy, we joined a support group of women who had used the sperm bank to become pregnant. Some of these women have become our friends, and our children now play together. (Until he went to preschool, Evan knew more families with two moms than families with a mom and a dad.)

This reminds me about the first time a preschool friend said, "So Evan, do you have a dad?" Pam and I had fretted about this moment. Would he be embarrassed, sad, traumatized? But he answered that question as if his friend had asked him, "So Evan, do you have a cat?"

"No," he answered calmly. "I have two women, two moms." After a silent sigh of relief, I talked with Evan and his friend about how some families have one parent, some have two; some have brothers, some have sisters.

Right after Evan was born I worried: Who would teach him to shave? How would he learn to pee standing up? Without a daily role model, would he know he was a boy and that he'd grow into a man? Now I don't worry about these things because I see that he is growing up like other boys his age. (Even with two pacifist mothers, he figured out how to make pretend guns out of Tinker Toys!)

One day, when he was just starting to use the toilet, I mentioned to him, "You know men usually stand up to pee and you will someday, too." The next day, as I walked by the bathroom, I saw him standing with his legs pressed against the toilet bowl, leaning over it with a look of fierce determination on his face. He is eager to grow into a man, and I imagine he'll ask his uncle to teach him how to shave when the time comes. He has a terrific mix of qualities: gentle, loving, cuddly, energetic, loud, and physical.

Many of the things I agonized over before are easier than I had anticipated. Our challenges now are like those of most families with young children: ear infections, temper tantrums, and childcare. But I still wonder what Evan will say if the barber asks him whether his haircut is like his father's. And I wonder how long I'll feel nervous when other parents in the park ask me what my husband looks like.

51 Harassment St.

Janice Wood

I'm convinced that people are actually hired to ride public transportation just to harass mothers traveling with their kids. How else to explain the intense interest in everything about us as we sit quietly on the 38 Geary? Too much air, too much sun, he should have a hat, I'm holding the bottle wrong, that stroller will ruin his back, where are his shoes?

Get a life, folks. This is none of your business.

I'm an older, adoptive mom. So when I first started riding the bus, I thought there might be something about me that made people wonder about my competence. But after a few weeks, as Matthew thrived and continued to be a happy, charming child who was obviously well taken care of, I started asking other moms about this public mama harassment.

It was true . . . there is an army of people out there who feel compelled, if not ordained, to give strident, judgmental advice to every parent they see. One friend who rode the bus in Manhattan while she was pregnant said she was so used to being poked and scolded during pregnancy, nothing could faze her once the child was born.

The advice comes screaming from everywhere. If you're ever feeling invisible, try walking down the street pushing a kid with one shoe missing in a stroller. . . . People yell from their windows, from buses, they stop their cars just to tell you the news.

One day I was pushing Matthew to daycare, and he had a particularly messy sneeze in the middle of a crosswalk. Before we got to the other side of Bush Street, some guy leaned out of his pickup and yelled, "Hey, clean that kid's nose!"

The stories are endless, perhaps only to be appreciated by other walking and bus-riding moms. Just recently, I literally had to flee from an umbrella-wielding crank who insisted that my son be smacked because he had been teasing me with a bus transfer.

It's all part of the same syndrome that allows people to feel they can poke and tickle and tousle the hair of kids they've never met, and offer them candy without even making eye contact with the parent. Matthew got so fed up with a couple of women who wouldn't keep their hands off him that he changed his seat. As they gave him one last poke on the way off the bus, laughing merrily as he tried to fend them off, he sputtered, "Shut up, you butt-butt girls," expressing his frustration quite eloquently, I thought.

Not everyone agreed about who was behaving badly, however. A young, probably childless man standing nearby looked at me and said, "Is he yours? You have my sympathy."

Most bus drivers aren't in on the public mama harassment. They tend to be helpful, or at least patient, often ordering another passenger to give "this lady" a seat.

But there was one grim day that still haunts me.

It was pouring rain, and the 4 Sutter driver was angry at me before we even got on the bus because he thought I was taking too long getting up the steps. As it happened, my stroller had been stolen the day before (yes, as I stood a few feet away, waiting for my bus). I had a neighbor's stroller, which took at least three people to fold up, so I asked if I couldn't leave it open for the few blocks we were going. A hostile look from the driver got me moving, and as I tried to fold up the rusty stroller and keep the baby from falling over in his seat, we continued to argue the point. Three other women on board took the driver's side and basically told me to shut up. One other woman sat frozen in her seat, either afraid to take sides or appalled by the whole scene.

Not one person helped me then, or when I finally got off a few blocks later. I felt like I'd already done a day's work before I even got to the office.

There have been the occasional kind words and helpful hints on the bus, and I have had plenty of good conversations I would have missed by traveling alone. I have found that elderly women are the most likely to help with getting the stroller off the bus or offer me a seat. Actually, middle-aged guys can be pretty helpful, but there aren't too many of them on the bus.

I have a car now, but Matthew and I still ride the bus when I don't feel like dodging UPS trucks and searching endlessly for a parking space. Matthew's met all colors and ages and shapes of people on the bus, heard dozens of languages, witnessed all degrees of kindness and meanness, and learned not to point and not to say, "She's fat!" or "He smells!" He's learned to read Stop Requested, Keep Arm In, and the dreaded Not In Service. He's also learned to say, with all his four-year-old might, "It's none of your business!" when told to take his thumb out of his mouth.

Matthew plans to be a bus driver when he grows up and has only to decide between the #42 and the #1 as his chosen line. He's promised that his bus sign will never say Garage and that he will help people and always wait for moms running with their kids.

Northern Mama

Sara Crangle

I t is the tail end of the darkest part of winter, a time when the sun
hits the top of the trees at around 10 A.M. and temperatures have
been hovering around -45 °C for the last three weeks. This cold
snap I have renamed cold trap: My daughter and I have spent long days
alone in our little cabin, struggling to keep warm, to be cheery company
for each other. Her biological father, who was here when she slid out
between my legs a year ago, now lives Outside, the northern name for
anyplace south of the 60th parallel. He left while the sun was still shin-
ing 16 hours a day. Thoughts of the impending darkness scared me then.
Now it is just me and her, my arm wrapped snugly around her at night
as she twists to be near me, near the breasts she thinks of as her own.
Together we are overcoming the dark.

Our cabin is 20 miles outside of Whitehorse in the Yukon Territory. It
is surrounded by a woodpile, an outhouse, endless miles of coniferous forest and mountains. The North is a part of the world where I am reminded
that gender is no measure of specific skills and abilities. Here women as
well as men are expected to be able to split wood, care for cantankerous
vehicles, haul water, and cook a fine moose stew. No special credit is given

to women who have overcome obstacles of upbringing and socialization to become adept at these things. It seems almost natural in this androgynous world of survival to be both mother and father to my child.

All winter I have mothered a child and a wood stove. On very cold days they feel like siblings vying for my attention. Sometimes they work in miraculous harmony: late-night feedings coinciding with the stove's hunger for another log or two. On mornings when the fire is dead and her hands are cold on my body, I stoke the coals, wrap the blankets from the bed around us, and bring her to honor the day's new flame. We sit on a chair and watch the flames dance, both of us motionless and fascinated. I love the immediacy of the wood heat, the way it penetrates our bones and makes our cheeks glow. Our heat source undeniably creates a great deal of work. Splitting wood is the only household task I can't do with my daughter on my back and I live in perpetual fear that one day I'll forget she's there when I'm in a hurry to get kindling.

I had no idea how important good friends and family would be after my daughter was born. My circle of friends has pulled in close around us, and I lean on them, each member in turn. On days when single parenting is more hard than sweet, I can count on them for gifts like a filled wood box, jugs of water and groceries from town, help with a flat tire, or beautiful moments alone in the bush while they hang out with my daughter. I see how her growth begins to amaze them as it amazes me. She crawls eagerly to meet them at the door, covered in dog hair and bits of bark stuck to her securely by the snow melting on the floor. She points insistently at our eternally shedding pet and says, "Da, da, da, da." She is a six-toothed wonder. She screws her eyes up tight and opens her smiling mouth wide to show off those teeth.

Recently I received a letter from down South, from an old friend/

lover. There was a flirtatious sentence in that letter that tugged at my ego. He knows you have a child and he wrote that anyway, I told myself. I sometimes long for the excitement of new romance, but I will be hard-pressed to find it in the isolated town where we live. Maybe I don't feel grounded enough as a parent to admit a third person into the equation. For now I will just stoke the stove and fill the hot-water bottle. For now it is enough to have a new life and old loves.

This past fall I drove to a friend's cabin, down a heavily rutted road lined with aspen trees that my headlights made eerie. We spent a cozy evening diverting my daughter from the wood stove and eating bowls and bowls of homemade soup. Later we went outside to watch the northern lights streak across the sky. I held my girl, bundled in an old wool blanket, up to the magnificent bolts of green and purple. "See the lights? See the lights?" The vast and mysterious spirits that beckon us here illuminate this vast and mysterious place to which we have become inextricably tied. The gifts this harsh land gives are plentiful. It gives me endless pleasure to have them be a part of her childhood and my adulthood. I love this part of the world, and I am not alone. Isolated, but not alone.

🖊️ Ask Yo Mama

You Have Questions, She Has Answers!

Dear Yo Mama,
I read your "Daybook" every season, and I voted for you
for president, but my friends say you are too militant. I don't
know what to think.

Think for yourself, girlfriend. I have been called militant,
hysterical, commie, and better. It doesn't bother me; you
can decide if it bothers you. In the meantime, rest assured
that "militant" means "weapons-oriented," and I'm a nonviolent kind of gal.

Yo Mama!
Help! I'm pregnant and my doctor says I have way too many
piercings!

Fear not. Doctors like to have cows over nothing. You do
have to take out your belly button piercing and have a
professional piercer replace it with a monofilament. You
may also want to remove labia and clit piercings for child-
birth and nipple piercings for nursing. Obviously, piercings
above the neck are irrelevant.

Dear Yo Mama,
My five-year-old daughter does not believe that I saw Star
Wars when I was younger and wanted to be like Luke Sky-
walker when I grew up, too! She says they couldn't possibly
have had Star Wars in the "olden days!" What should I do?

Hold your ground—but ask yourself, Is this "olden days"
stuff bringing up other issues for me?

Dear Yo Mama,
Were you in Wal-Mart in Austin, Texas, a few months back?
I could've sworn I saw you.

No, I haven't been to Austin in a while. That must've been Drew Barrymore.

Dear Yo Mama,
I can't get my four-year-old to eat the food I make. Help!

Contrary to popular belief, a kid never starved with a plate full of food in front of him.

Dear Yo Mama,
My baby's new daddy, my lover, my sweetheart, turns to face me as we leave a party. He tells me I am beautiful, that I dress well, that he's proud to show me off to his friends. Proud to objectify me and proud of the way I've objectified myself. With class. With ambition. With one smooth black chopstick holding my swirled hair to the back of my head and with my too-tall shoes, I've become an ornament. His decoration. He tells me all this with one look. This is the only time I've been able to read his eyes. I feel good because I wanted to be beautiful. I feel relieved to be perceived as a beautiful woman, but it makes me feel like a girl. Like a child. I feel like an elaborate blowup doll. I feel like nothing. My boyfriend is like heaven. He is sweet and strong and funny and he loves me. My daughter screams for him. He is never malicious or unkind. The problem is, I cannot explain to him who I am. When I speak to him another voice flies from my mouth. I quote my mother, my sister, old lovers, and roommates I never even liked. I'm cryptic and my behavior

is strange when he's around. There was a woman at the party. She was not beautiful when you first looked at her, but she became my definition of beauty by 1 A.M. She told tall tales and was going to ride her bike around the world in the year 2000. I fell in love with her (even with the ends of her hair, crimpy from a bad permanent). She understood me by the time I left the party and I understood her. This has happened before with me and women and has not happened with men. Am I gay? Is this how all relationships are with men, even perfect men, two separate people spending time together? Help!

Hmmmmm . . . why not hook up with the girl? Or . . . ask Isadora!

Dear Yo Mama,
I had to work a double shift the other day, I hadn't eaten anything but a candy bar all day, and then when I got home the baby would not go to sleep. I tried to comfort him, tried to feed him, tried every mama trick I had up my sleeve, but by 4 A.M. I screamed (really loudly), "I am going to fucking die!" Am I a bad mother?

I am working on banishing the phrase "bad mother" from the English language. Under the circumstances, "I am going to fucking die" was a pretty good thing to yell. (Much better than "I am going to kill you," for example.) Babies get stressed when we are stressed because they pick up on our feelings. Maybe you could think up a few good phrases to yell that won't end up making you feel bad for future use . . . try "Republicans are evil!" or something. Anyway, too much yelling around the house can scare a baby, but don't worry about it. You are human. You are mama. You may roar sometimes! So just try to eat enough healthy food, don't accept double shifts if you can help it, and keep on keepin' on.

Dear Yo Mama,
Are you really planning to overthrow the government?

I think I have a few things on my calendar before that.

Dear Yo Mama,
I seem to have lost my mind. Have you seen it?

I think I saw one wandering by about an hour ago, but it was in pretty sorry condition. I wouldn't bother chasing it if I were you.

Dear Yo Mama,
Who are you? And where do you live?

I am a mama. I have a functioning brain and many unexplained capabilities. I frighten right-wing dittoheads because I speak the truth. I live everywhere and nowhere.
Yo Mama

Anonymous Was a Mother

Anonymous AKA Marcy Sheiner

For some years now I've hovered around the edge of a group of people who call themselves "sex radicals" or "the sex community," people who write, think, and philosophize about sex, fight censorship on many different fronts, and engage in unorthodox behavior like public and group sex. I got here, as most people do, by accident, on a journey that began when I first used my pen to write pornography for profit and fun (in that order).

While to the outside world the "sex radical" community is seen as hedonistic and decadent, we see what we're doing as social justice work that will ultimately lead to a freer, more humane society. Many believe that the path to spiritual enlightenment is through sexual excess, or at least exploration. They see themselves as daring pioneers engaged in a fight whose consequences are as significant for themselves and for future generations as, say, the French and Russian Revolutions.

But I don't feel like a daring pioneer for writing about sex. For me, the scariest place to venture with my pen has always been into the territory of motherhood.

As the mother of two adult children, one of whom was born with a chronic medical condition, I've made sporadic attempts to write honestly about my experience for more than 30 years. I got stuck in rage, I got stuck in terror—but most of all I got stuck in the writer's hell of self-censorship. I knew that if I told the truth about what motherhood has been like for me, I would be breaking a taboo much stronger than the one against sexual expression. I would be violating a conspiracy of silence that serves to keep the human race propagating. Furthermore, if I wrote about how difficult motherhood has been for me, I would open myself to the irrational charge, frequently leveled against mothers who deviate in any way from the norm, that I don't sufficiently love my children. If I told the truth, without couching it in good-natured jokes—that for me motherhood has been more of a source of pain than pleasure—I would be seen as defective, unnatural, inhuman. Worst of all, if my children were to read what I wrote, I would, even at this late date, do them irreparable harm. I would be vulnerable to the most deadly epithet known to woman: "a bad mother." And so, ironically, while I have signed my real name to most of my pornography, it is only under the time-honored byline of "Anonymous" that I finally feel free to write about motherhood.

I'm no stranger to artistic criticism. As a porn writer, I've received my share of social censure, including being called a bad mother: After all, what kind of mother lets her kids—and in the public domain, yet—know that she's sexually active? My work has been condemned, if not specifically, then in its collective genre. Mostly it's been trivialized, laughed at, dismissed by friends and family as a good way to make a buck. While many of my colleagues go ballistic over such attitudes, I remain relatively undisturbed by them: While I think these attitudes are absurd, they don't twist my guts in the same way as do attacks on mothers.

Things were pretty rough when I had my first baby 30 years

ago, and though styles have changed, as far as I can tell the behavior of mothers is still subject to greater scrutiny than that of any other class of human beings on the planet. Witness the current suggestion of criminalizing women who take drugs during pregnancy, the latest manifestation of control over women's bodies and behavior. Nobody wants to see babies born addicted to crack—but what's next? Sugar? Coffee? Failure to exercise sufficiently, as determined by the latest trendsetting fitness guru?

Personally, I have been criticized, directly or indirectly, for doing something to cause my son's disability; denying my son's disability; making too much of my son's disability; overfeeding; incorrect feeding; inattentiveness; incompetence; writing when I should have been earning money; working when I should have been home; writing about sex; not writing enough about my children; writing too much about my son and not enough about my daughter; letting my kids live with their father; taking them back; drinking and dancing in front of my kids; endangering them by living in the city; depriving them by living in the country; being a lax disciplinarian; being insufficiently involved in their schoolwork; interfering with their autonomy; dressing inappropriately for a mother; being open about my sexuality; letting lovers sleep over; being bisexual; having a long-term black lover and including him in family activities; speaking and writing on political issues; surrounding my kids with unusual kinds of people; subjecting them to communal living; depriving them of a normal family life; emasculating my son with feminism; compromising feminist events by bringing my son along; imparting sexist attitudes; foisting nonsexist attitudes on them; failing to give them religion; failing to inspire patriotism; favoring my son; favoring my daughter; being open about who I am; not moving on with my life when my kids were old enough; being selfish about my time when, after all, they still needed me; enabling; overprotecting; neglecting; and just plain fucking up.

These criticisms came from my mother; my sister and other relatives; my ex-husband; his mother and other in-laws; friends; lovers; my women's consciousness-raising group; my women's theater group; employers; co-workers; doctors; teachers; social workers; therapists; bank tellers; shop-keepers; strangers in the park; and, most recently, my daughter. They also came, less directly, from television, newspapers, magazines, and books. When an outside critic wasn't on the case, I did the job myself.

No wonder mothers have written so little and so superficially on the subject: Whatever we can say can and will be used against us in or out of a court of law. And then there are more benign reasons why mothers don't write of their experiences. In *Of Woman Born,* Adrienne Rich confessed that the reason she so rarely wrote about her children was that her writing was the one place she could get away from them. There's also the practical matter of time: Mothers simply don't have it, and by the time the kids are grown we want to do something else already.

But I think that mothers have remained silent primarily out of fear. We are not supposed to feel ambivalence. We are not supposed to have negative feelings about motherhood, let alone negative feelings toward our children. And yet, when Ann Landers asked the question, "If you had it to do over again, would you have children?" 70 percent of her re-spondents said no. This statistic stunned me, since I only know two other women who have voiced these sentiments.

A few years ago, I put out a call for written materials from mothers, hoping to put together an anthology. I asked mothers of grown children to tell what it was like for them to raise their kids, pointedly asking for a focus on struggle. What I received were dozens of essays describing how

Johnny learned to read, or the happy-chaotic six-kid household. The few writers who did mention hardship made sure to conclude that "it was all worth it."

This hypocrisy has made me feel isolated, freakish, deprived of an allegedly joyful experience. I've felt like a witch, a Medea, an evil pariah. Like the Catholic who sins and then goes to confession for exoneration, I absolve my sins with self-castigation.

And just what are these sins? That I haven't lived up to anyone's standard of maternal perfection, certainly. But deeper still is the pain, which feels somehow sinful, of not having enjoyed what is touted as the greatest show on earth. Because I've been told that the experience of motherhood should be my deepest source of happiness, my dissatisfaction with it engenders profound suffering.

It should not be necessary to state this, but part of the problem is that I must: I dearly love my children and do not wish them gone. As a matter of fact, it is precisely the love I feel for these people, a complex, many-faceted love unparalleled by any other I have known, that makes the condition of motherhood so unbearable. That I can never do right by them, that they can never live a pain-free existence, that I unthinkingly caused some of their pain, that the world I brought them into isn't good enough for them—all these are sources of anguish to me.

I believe that most mothers—most parents—feel at least some of this.

Because my first child was born with a life-threatening chronic condition, these feelings have been intensified; from the start they overshadowed the pleasure experienced by most new parents. This situation strongly affected my attitude about motherhood and my behavior toward both my children. To this day it affects my relationship with them.

When I was abruptly informed of my first baby's condition, I had no idea what it was or what it would mean. But I instinctively knew that the world I had inhabited for 19 years would never look the same again. It hasn't. But it is only now, 30 years later and under the cover of "anonymous," that I am beginning to talk about just what it does look like.

This essay is lovingly signed by the one and only . . . Marcy Sheiner, coming out of the anonymous closet for this book because "in the struggle between vanity and circumspection, vanity has won out": "In publishing this piece again and under my name, I must reiterate: I never hated my children; what I hated was being oppressed as a mother in the myriad ways that American contemporary culture manages to oppress mothers."

Why Get Pregnant?

Recently, a single friend of mine mentioned that she was thinking about getting pregnant. It's the kind of comment I have trouble passing up without sharing my opinion. With this particular friend, I didn't have to consider it for long. She should.

She nodded. All the single moms she knew had told her the same thing, but the married moms cautioned her—it would be too hard alone. "I think maybe the hard thing is having a husband," she whispered.

I've never been married, so I know very little about the ease or difficulty of having a husband, but I was relieved that my friend didn't ask me to explain the advice I'd offered. Why do I think she should get pregnant? I would have drawn a blank and ended up giving her some cynical answer like "misery loves company." We can all think of a million reasons not to get pregnant. But, really, why should she get pregnant? Why should anyone?

On Mother's Day, almost a week after considering my friend's fate, I was in 7-Eleven buying a newspaper. A woman stood over a small child who was screaming for purple Now and Laters. The woman looked at me with tired eyes: "Remind me why I wanted to be a mother."

Of course, I couldn't.

Over the years, in various contexts, I've come up with many a lame reason for having kids. In jest: "I thought it would be cool to experience the effects of chronic sleep deprivation." In the welfare office after a six-hour wait: "To collect the generous cash grant, of course." In a bad speech: "So I'd stay out of trouble." In competition: "Because I knew I could do a better job than my (circle one: mother/sister/neighbor)." In an instant of chamomile tea–induced bliss holding a sleeping babe: "For moments like these." (Someone get the Kodak people here!)

Sure, we can point to all those intense moments burned into our memories that made it all feel worthwhile—first steps, adorable songs, amazement at the span of a duck's wings, glimpses of true love. But even monks experience moments of enlightenment if they go without sleep for long enough. And enlightenment, I suspected, would hardly satisfy the woman at 7-Eleven.

Being the sort of person I am—a little obsessive and unable to give up a good philosophical question—I decided I'd just have to come up with a good answer.

So, the next time I was in 7-Eleven, I asked one woman with a child why she got pregnant, and another who was buying condoms why she didn't want to. Both women looked at me like I was totally insane, paid for their Slurpees and rubbers, and left quickly.

Back home, I turned to my bookshelf. A few scientists and psychologists claim that the continuation of the species is the point. A valid one, depending upon your opinion of the species. Others claim a more narcissistic motive—children, ideally, are little mirrors. My book on Jung is not indexed, so I can only guess what he says. Maya Angelou says that pregnant women can experience "exquisite gratification." And Oriana Fallaci says that if you have children, then when you die, you don't really die.

On the phone I discovered that no one I know really had any idea why they had kids, either, but the most popular responses were "I felt like I had a lot to give," "I always wanted to be a mother," "I think it was a spiritual need," "Get some sleep, Ariel," and "Can I call you back?"

I'll admit that I sort of hoped my daughter would do something really awesome while I was trying to write this column so I could end with a cheesy vignette that summed it all up, but she spent the day exchanging bratty comments with a neighbor kid, and she's been sleeping all night. Maybe I had a child so I wouldn't have time to ponder the great mysteries of life. Maybe it's time to have another.

—Ariel

Letters to the Editor

The Other "F" Word

Ariel Dear,

The last Hip Mama was very interesting—the only objection for me was the "fart" word. That is my most detested word. I hate it as much as the other "F" word. But at my age I get to have a few peculiarities. Give Maia a kiss for me. I love you. xxx.

Evelyn Garrett (The editor's grandma)
San Clemente, California

How Old Are You?

I'm so impressed! Hip Mama is fantastic! Thank you for putting together such an honest, fun, cool zine. I could relate to the "How old are you?" thing. I'm 26, but I look like I'm about 18, and people look at me like it's a crime and/or a shame for me to have two kids. Even if I was 18, I think I'd deserve a bit more credit than that. I really love Hip Mama for the fact that it is so inclusive, so respectful of mamas of all ages and types. Keep up the good work!

Gayle Brandeis
Riverside, California

Reorient

Hip Mama,

Have you ever noticed how hard it is these days to figure out a) where the hell you are, b) how the hell you got there, and c) how the hell to get anywhere else???

I'm sure Hip Mama is going to reorient me.

Victoria DeMara

Berkeley, California

Toddlers in the Podium

Dear Mama,

My daughter Annie Dove and I had a chance to meet you at Powell's Bookstore in Portland a few days ago. Thank you for being okay with all the toddlers running around during your reading! I wished I had a camera to take a picture of all the little ones climbing on, under, and through the podium next to you.

I love your zine—it's a relief to have a voice that is real and chucks the pretense. Thank you.

Mama Sara Kirschenbaum

Portland, Oregon

Portrait of the Artist as a Young Mom

Sunday	Monday	Tuesday	Wednesday
1 Host baby shower for Jodie Foster. She doesn't show up!	**2** Drown sorrows in Rocket Espresso. Apologize to therapist.	**3** Get telemarketing pitch for Intergalactic Travel Service.	**4** Spend night in cornfield observing strange metallic object.
8 Take kids to various fathers for visits. Go out for Indian food with the mamas.	**9** Zine staff gets food stamp cut-off notices. Off they go to real jobs.	**10** Kids host Barney Roast complete with "Dead Barney" punk band.	**11** Therapist seems skeptical about aliens but sez: "I can hear that."
15 Take kids to various fathers for visits. Go platform shoe shopping.	**16** Get hate mail from fundamentalists who say I'll burn in hell.	**17** Go to Berkeley party; people greet each other: "Are you being persecuted?"	**18** Get abducted by aliens again. Return home with cut & bleached hair.
22 Take kids to various fathers for visits. Work all day.	**23** Kids wear underpants on heads for Dead Barney's rehearsal.	**24** Kids write new band song, "Tough Luck Titanic." Is this dysfunction?	**25** Therapist wants to explore Jodie Foster/Alien connection.
29 Take kids to various fathers for visits. Go see *The Wedding Singer.*	**30** Get soundtrack to listen to Adam Sandler sing "Somebody Kill Me."		

Thursday	Friday	Saturday
5 Get abducted by aliens along with 23 other bystanders.	**6** Return home unharmed except for strange new tattoo on belly.	**7** Neighborhood girls start Spice Girls fan club to terrorize me.
12 Buy "relaxing" & "revitalizing" bath salts. Probably should just sleep.	**13** Get accused of taking kids to Ani DiFranco show in family court. "Is that illegal?"	**14** Kids drag me to see *Spice World*. Wear hat & sunglasses.
19 Take shoebox to accountant. Get lecture about retirement.	**20** Accountant calls: Do I have receipts from Intergalactic Travel Service?	**21** Spice Girls proclaimed "out." Girls start retro Bangles fan club.
26 Restock Rocket Espresso supply. Work all night while kids watch *Grease*.	**27** Bangles declared "out." Neighborhood girls start L7 fan club.	**28** Dead Barney's playlist includes "Mama's gone Mental."

yo mama's daybook

The Ultimate Creative Prompt

Soo Young Lee

I am a statistic. I am a woman of color and I am a single mother. If you take the time to get to know me, you will see a woman who became a single mother by choice and a woman who is as complex and interesting as a 10-page menu at a fusion restaurant.

People often give me this pitying look when they find out I am a single mother. This is doubly so when they find out I am working on a book. The look then comes with a gesture—a hand on my shoulder, a gentle touch of my hand, a hand resting on a chin thoughtfully for a moment. They say things like, "It must be incredibly hard to sacrifice all your time for your child." They make comments about how they can hardly take care of themselves, let alone someone else, or how they are too busy to work on their own art. I do not take their condescending commentary personally. Maybe my determination makes them question their own complacency. What they do not understand is that in some ways motherhood fosters art and creative expression. Yes, as mothers, we struggle with sleep deprivation, multitasking to extremes, and major boundary issues. But for mothers, writing or finding a creative outlet becomes more essential. We need written, musical, and artistic reminders and records of who we were and who we are evolving into. It becomes a necessity because it can easily feel like you are losing touch with the woman who existed before the diapers and the ugly pastel diaper bags. Salvation comes in those slices of time when your child is asleep or at the sitter's, and you can find your dim corner with the desk lamp haloing your laptop. When you are childless, everything from your shoes to your favorite bar is an easy expression of who you are as an individual. My childless friends can spend time worrying about if their hair is too short, if last year's winter coat reflects who they want to be this year, or whether they should make the switch from dress shoes to sneakers. These issues of visual identity and self-expression become quite complicated after conception. Many changes are completely beyond your control: Your breasts become milk bottles, your smooth flat belly becomes a house (a fleshy igloo of sorts). Even my tattoos have been claimed by my son as his pictures. I think children have a survival instinct that can turn into a Genghis Khan–esque ambition to conquer and take over your life, complete with sloppy kisses. We argue over a box of crayons and art supplies.

He says, "These are not yours, they are ours."

With gritted teeth as I grab back my box of French watercolor pencils, I say, "Tristan, some things are not shared. Some things are just mine."

Then the dictator replies, "Yes, but these are ours because it is nice to share, Mommy."

So, by the end of the day or beginning of the day, it is beneficial to have claimed and asserted a sense of self. If I can begin and finish a piece of writing before I pick him up at school, I can be the best mom in the world. I can smile and laugh without thinking about the guilt plaguing me to do something just for myself. I will not fear his neediness or desire for my attention. I don't feel like he is trying to suck away my energy, because I am fortified with my writing and creative expression. At some point, I began to realize that these notions of feeling drained and ebbed away came from myself, not from the child. They are just flights of nightmarish fancy because they disappear—"poof"—like magic after a session of writing or two hours at the gym. But I don't underestimate how thoughts can create reality if I let them. I think this often happens in any close relationship, whether it is with a child or with a lover who seems to suddenly turn into an ugly, demanding toad instead of the lovely prince or princess you opened your heart and body to. The difference between a break from your lover and a break from your child is that with a child, you cannot sleep at your own apartment the next day because the child lives with you for 18 years and then some.

I am also motivated by the desire to not be a hypocrite. You know how parents encourage you to do and be whatever you want because they believe in you. Statements like "I know you can do anything you put your mind to" or "Choose a career that uses your full potential and dreams" mean nothing without some backing. Children learn from living example, and it is difficult to live up to the advice that we give to our children. That is why the saying "Do as I say, not as I do" is so popular. As parents we all know the grain of truth this saying holds. It is daunting for us to realize how much our actions will influence our children. It makes us want to laugh nervously at the truth of it. But as a child, how do you accept the motto "Live your dreams" when your own parents are working jobs they hate with a passion? Jobs that force them to tune out during the week and look forward to flipping channels on their multichannel satellite service, so they can tune out some more. I want to tell my son, "Go for the architecture degree if you want to because you made fabulous Lego buildings at the age of two." I want to show him the pictures of the massive colorful structures of the windmill, museum, and spaceship that he made at six. I can't help but believe that this kind of advice will hold more weight if I am a working writer or at least enjoying my job and feeling like I have given something of myself to this world.

Having a precocious child also contributes to my writing. He is always questioning the meaning of words and how I use them. He makes me realize how words affect my perception of the world. He always wants to know what words mean and wants an example to go along with it.

"I need to discipline myself," I say to my friend over tea at the local coffee shop.

My son with his big ears asks while peering over his steamer, "What is dis-ip-pline?"

I reply without a thought, "Umm . . . it's learning to do something you do not like, so that you can get to something good later."

He says that doesn't make sense.

I give an example: "Let's say you are training for a marathon, but you don't want to train and run because it is hard. Well, it will be hard to run well at the race because you did not discipline yourself for it."

"Ugh, sounds like no fun," he says.

I lay awake that night because I think about how I presented discipline as something ugly and loathsome because I felt it was. I turn over this image again and again of him becoming a long-haired slacker with no direction and no muscle tone.

I used to hate the words "self-control" and "discipline." But the last few years have made me realize how impossible it is to produce anything without making the time to be available to your craft. You can have all the silk-covered notebooks of ideas to write from, but without the work and process of writing, they are just nice decorations for the coffee table. As the sun came up, I thought of new ways to approach this word with him.

After cooking him his favorite breakfast, I sweetly said, "Disciplining is loving the hard and fun parts of getting to a goal or dream."

He looked up at me with a mouth full of chocolate chip pancakes and mumbled, "Stop comfusing muh, Mum."

It was too late. From then on, I had to make double sure that I tried to walk my talk with him. This meant writing when I said I would instead of checking my email for an hour. He makes me accountable to my craft, so much more than any editor or deadline because he lives with me and witnesses my everyday actions.

One day we were reading a book that had the word "capitalism" in it.

He asked me about that word, and I told him that it is a system of money that creates a very poor group and a very rich group in the world.

My friend Iowaka overheard us and said, "Don't you think that is a bit biased?"

I had no idea what she was talking about.

She told him that it is a system of exchange where goods are traded for money.

But he just shook his head, refusing to listen to her. So I'd planted a socialist seed in his head. Maybe that is the power of first words and first meanings—once they are implanted and imparted from someone you love a great deal, they provide the blueprint of the word and the blueprint for how that word will shape you. This is a powerful exchange. As a mother, you help to create the physical child. But as the purveyor of early vocabulary, you help to mold his or her personalities and perceptions.

My socialist, slacker son may be forever affected by my use of words and vocabulary. The damage and gifts will be imparted, and he will struggle with his own meanings and viewpoints someday.

But I have learned something in our exchange, too. I realize again the gift and power of words. I rejoice in my ability to find nuances of meaning and discover new similes. "My pen waited to bleed on the page like the breastmilk responding to a baby's cry." These maternal comparisons came from my primal desire to preserve and discover myself, which surfaced mostly after motherhood. They were an unexpected gift that came with the leaking breast pads, puffy eyes, loss of self, and finding of self.

My son had very bad colic, which kept both of us up throughout the night. I remember one Sunday night when he was two, I cried myself to sleep because I felt so lost and shapeless within the boundaries and markings of motherhood. I had no idea where my personal dreams went or how to find my libido.

The next morning, I woke up at dawn and started writing to save my life as a woman, as an artist. This writing came from a frantic, possessed place. At first it was just remembering how to move the pen across the paper again and again, longer than the time it takes to write a to-do list or fill out a check. I created another kind of list where I wrote down what I wanted for myself from that moment on. I wrote things like "a morning to myself to watch the sun come up in the quiet of the house" and "long conversations with adults about adult subjects." I found myself laughing and slowly felt the transformation. Then it came, what I was waiting for after an hour of laboring over my notepad. A poem about broken branches, iridescent beetles, rhyme and coupling—and the most amazing thing—the lines came trembling out of my hand, and I realized how necessary this exercise was.

I Shouldn't Feel This Guilt

June Day

My daughter is almost two. I have not produced any significant artwork or writing since her birth. I no longer call myself a writer, even in secret. I catch myself confessing to old friends at galleries and independent films, "I'm just being a mother right now—she's still so little. . . ." Their looks confirm my own suspicions: I'm a lame white-trash welfare leech.

For the last three mornings my daughter has been getting up before 3 A.M., instead of her usual 6 A.M. I'm developing a twitch in my right eye. She takes a two-hour nap, which is when I do the dishes, clean, pay bills, and brainstorm about how to make lunch out of one can of government-issue corn and three gallons of WIC milk. I spend my creativity with this can of corn, not a paintbrush. Most days, when I try to hold my daughter's hand, or help her with a puzzle or a utensil, she cries, "No, Mommy, I dood it!" More energy spent trying to stay grown-up when I want to scream, "Mine!"

The thing is, I feel awful all around. When I try to do art, it sucks. I'm not there with it. I'm a full-time mom, which is great, but it sometimes sucks, too. Mothering is really, really hard. I never get enough sleep; I'm always stressed; I have zits; and I can't afford a haircut; gas for my car, fresh fruit, or Band-Aids.

My guilt over being "unproductive" tires me out. I shouldn't feel this guilt. I shouldn't have to. The source of my problem is in cultural expectations of me. It isn't enough just to be a mother, even though it's difficult and important. Good motherhood isn't considered successful or even sufficient. One must have a MotherPlus Plan—maybe have the MotherPlus law career or be a MotherPlus novelist. It fills me with guilt, always coming up short.

I have to remind myself that giving a little person a fabulous life is enough. Sometimes she reminds me herself by pretending to be a small sheep and saying "Baaaa" while she nudges her cheek against mine. Suddenly everything shifts; writing is some distant hobby and my girl is a sweet little fairy who has chosen me to follow and lead about. I stop pressuring her to eat fried, microwaved, or broiled corn, and we skip about the apartment laughing hysterically. When she's older, she may choose not to behave like a drunken monkey, so I'd better hang out with her now.

News Flash

Ironing Boards Found to Be Obsolete

Americans are losing their zest for cleaning, according to a recent study of national attitudes toward cleaning by Black & Decker, makers of the DustBuster. The study found that fully 20 percent of women and 24 percent of men are "anti-cleaners," who, like *Hip Mama*'s own chaotic editor, would do almost anything to avoid cleaning the house.

Another 21 percent of women and 23 percent of men are "reluctant cleaners."

According to Black & Decker, wash-and-wear and dry-clean-only clothes have rendered the iron almost obsolete.

Most people think nothing of tossing dirty laundry in the closet, sweeping dirt under the rug, or "just shutting the door when company comes."

Only about one-third of women described themselves as "Felix Unger types," or total clean freaks. Then there were those who identified themselves as "stream-of-consciousness cleaners" who clean "on the fly with no particular pattern." This group included about twice as many men as women.

The average American household has two vacuum cleaners and six to seven other "cleaning tools," such as paper towel holders, rags, and dustpans, all of which are seldom used.

How I Became a Cartoonist

Katherine Arnoldi

When I started *The Amazing True Story of a Teenage Single Mom,* I wasn't thinking of a book at all. All I wanted to do was learn how to become a cartoonist. I took out a blank sheet of paper and decided to concentrate first on the drawing. I'll just tell the story of my life, I thought, and that way I won't have to think about the words.

I started with the most life-changing event, the moment my daughter was born, and told my day-to-day life one panel at a time. I didn't think anyone would ever see these drawings, so I felt free to experiment with different styles and assuage my fears about drawing by making elaborate borders. One thing I noticed right away: As I drew the pictures of my past, the memories came barreling back in a different way than when I had written about these experiences. It was as though the memory came through my arm and appeared before me like a movie.

Often I would find myself at my drawing table, my body racked with sobs at seeing images of myself as a young teenage mom: on my way to work at the factory, carrying a baby, a diaper bag, a purse, and my lunch out to the car in the dead of night, having to leave my daughter at a daycare center and then being overwhelmed all day by her cries when I left her. Seeing myself being battered by a boyfriend and realizing, when I drew my child in the next room, a prisoner in her highchair, the horrible instability that she was being subjected to. As I drew, I saw more deeply the truth of my memories, and, I realized, the truth of other single moms and their children. As I worked, I had sympathy for the character of myself. I saw how I had struggled with such a limited knowledge of the world—how, at a time when many teenagers are thinking about what they want to be when they grow up and how they will accomplish that, I was thinking about whether I had enough money to buy the number of baby food jars I needed to last until the next paycheck and then living with the realization that I did not.

Time and again I was shocked to see the reality of my life there before me, irrefutably stark. I started one drawing with the words, "I tiptoed down the stairs." And as I drew my feet on the stairs, the memory came back to me, as though bursting through my arm. When I was finished, I saw the exact steps, the exact house that was a suppressed and forgotten nightmare. I drew my arms holding up a chair, ready to hit my brother-in-law over the back. I drew myself on the floor of the room that was mine while I lived with my brother-in-law and my sister, sketching a chair propped up against the doorknob to keep my brother-in-law out, and remembered that the room was only as wide as the door. As I kept drawing panel after panel, I suddenly realized: This is the story of my struggle to go to college; this is the story of how I found Jackie Ward, another single mom, who told me about financial aid and the possibility that even I could go to college. At the time that I began the cartoon, I was running a program at Charas Community Center on Ninth Street and Avenue B called the Single Mom College Program, where I would hand out financial aid and college applications. I was trying to do for others what Jackie had done for me. I would also go to GED programs where I was shocked to learn that single moms graduated without ever being told about the process of applying and the advantages of going to college.

On my trips to the GED programs, I began to notice a disturbing fact. Just because single moms had the application, and even though they told me they wanted to go to college, most did not fill out the applications right there with me, as I'd hoped. Instead, they politely excused themselves, said they had to run to pick up their children, and, often forgetting their applications, ran out the door, waving to me, repeatedly thanking me for coming.

Something was wrong.

I realized that the problem was not just that they lacked the information. The problem was the same problem I had had: They didn't feel worthy to use it. Shockingly, even though it was the 1990s, these single moms felt that they, too, had made their bed and had to lie in it, that they had made a "mistake" that had made them ineligible to participate in the world. In fact, their feelings of unworthiness were even more severe than mine had been. These women had been bombarded with anti-welfare rhetoric, with propaganda poised to discourage teen pregnancy by attacking teen moms themselves. I felt I could discern on their faces the same feeling I had had as a teen mom, the feeling that I had ruined my life, but there was more there: These women had the added burden of being made scapegoats for the economic difficulties of the early 1990s. It was they, not Desert Storm or the savings and loan bailout or global changes, who had caused the nation's economic problems.

All they wanted was to disappear. How well I understood that!

The journey between having a pen in hand and putting it to the application form for these women is an epic one, filled with as many demons, monsters, temptations, and obstacles as any superhero story. As I drew the story of that period of my life, I realized I was making a cartoon book about my own struggles to feel worthy, to put the pen to paper, to move from a life of limitations—of wanting to be invisible—to a life of possibilities.

It was my friend Jackie, a single mom with two children, who had helped me traverse the great divide, who had somehow convinced me that not only was I worthy, but education was a right I was being denied and that I had to fight for. Jackie had empowered me enough that when I got to the University of Arkansas and they denied me financial aid, I marched over to the legal aid office and returned with my lawyer. The grant that I was told there was "no way" I could get suddenly became available. But how many had been turned away?

I began to see my cartoon book as a way to do for single moms what Jackie had done for me. I photocopied it, stapled copies together, and handed them out at GED programs and at my readings. "The perfect gift for the single mom in *your* family," I ranted.

As time passed, though, I became discouraged. Several friends made fun of my interest in single moms, telling me I needed "to wake up and smell the _____," that I should get on with my life, or, actually, "get a life." I was a writer; what I needed was a novel, they said.

I kept working on the cartoon book, kept going to GED programs, kept my dream. I just stopped talking about it so much. Feelings of unworthiness again overwhelmed me. In a positive moment, I took out the cartoon book and took it to my agent, Jennifer Hengen. She had called me many years before and wanted to represent me after reading a piece I wrote in *Fiction*. She had been patiently waiting for a novel. Instead I gave her the cartoon book.

She sent it out and got an offer. It looked like *The Amazing True*

Story of a Teenage Single Mom might have a chance to reach not only those I could take copies to, but truly the single mom in *your* family.

I sent a letter to Jackie to tell her the good news. I did not hear back. Finally, I called. Her husband answered the phone. Jackie had been killed in a car accident several months before. Although she had seen the little photocopied copy of the book and knew of my gratitude, of how she changed my life, she would never know how her acts of generosity, her patience toward my feelings of unworthiness, and her insistence that I had an equal right to education would, like a ripple or some divine pyramid scheme for good, affect first me, then maybe more than either of us could have dreamed.

Maybe there'll be a national bring-your-child-to-class day to protest the lack of daycare. Maybe there'll be a bring-your-child-to-the-dorms day. Maybe single moms will go en masse to college.

My daughter, the little girl imprisoned in the highchair, traumatized in the beginning of the book, chooses to see herself on the back of the bike, in paroxysms of giggles and laughter, while her mother speeds off to college classes. She chooses to wonder, too, what her purpose might be, what contribution she might make. She is hoping to find the happiness of a meaningful life. She wants to give her own children not beds to lie in, but a feeling of worthiness and footsteps to step into and then out of, going as far as their potential will allow, as far as their purpose might lead them.

A Case for the Countryside

Leslie Gore

My son does not know about frozen spinach. He does not squirm, as I do, when our next-door neighbor goes out to the rabbit hutch, knocks a fluffy bunny on the back of the head, skins it in one gesture, and brings it in to us ready for the evening stew. Anyone who eats, kills.

Maybe we don't give enough of our blood back to the earth. Maybe that's why we need war. Words are not the same thing as what they describe.

Without any encouragement from me, my son, when we were walking through the woods near our house, understood the importance of finding his first porcupine quill. No camera flash, no Kodak, just a face. A porcupine quill is something.

Why do I live out in the country among all the rednecks and silly hippies? Why do I put up with the isolation and having to drive so many kilometers just to work, to study, or to shop?

It is about living inside your body and knowing what your body is made of.

It is about real power and where that comes from.

It is about singing even if no one hears you.

News Flash

Pop Music Good for Studies

Studying to loud pop music may help children in school. At least that's what British researchers found when they divided 11,000 children into three groups to listen to a pop radio station, classical music, and a discussion program.

On IQ tests, the kids listening to Top 40 music came out with scores 4 percent higher than the other groups'. "I think this is an emotional effect," said researcher Sue Hallam of London's Institute of Education. "The children enjoyed [the pop tunes] and were motivated."

Motoring with Mary

Molly Gove Interviews Mary Water

ary Water grew up working-class in Rutherford, New Jersey, and left home at age 17 to go to the Evergreen State College in Olympia, Washington. Mary got pregnant right after her first year at school and gave birth to Random at age 19. She made her first tape, a musical story called "Happy Halloween," when Random was eight months old.

In 1998, when Random was three, Mary's band Little Red Car Wreck released an album dubbed *Motor Like a Mother.*

My friend Sarah told me about Mary and Little Red Car Wreck. So one morning after dropping my own three-year-old daughter, Hugo, off at preschool I rode my bike down to the record shop and sat in a sound booth listening to the CD from start to finish. If anyone had peeked in the window they would have seen me alternately crying, laughing, covered in chill bumps, and mostly smiling bigtime. So I plopped down $13.99 of the grocery money and took the CD home. The songs are steeped in the imagery and themes of motherhood: dishes, laundry, welfare, car seats, and a force of will as strong as a motor.

Molly: How did your folks react to your pregnancy?

Mary: I think my mom introduced it to my dad by saying, "What's the worst thing you can possibly imagine happening?" And the worst was me being addicted to heroin and next was me being pregnant.

Molly: Was there ever a feeling that you wouldn't be able to do music with a kid? What's been hard?

Mary: I wasn't really playing shows before Random was born, so it was really hard to get started. But that's the thing I find about kids: They give you this direction that is so clear, they show you where your direction is going to be. Even though things get really hard it's like when I used to run cross-country in high school—I was able to run much better when I was going uphill. When things are really hard I just am able to do them better. I usually get really depressed in the summer here, but not in the winter because there is something to struggle against. I remember all of these times practicing and Random screaming at my leg, totally hysterical, and me saying, "Five more minutes." Sometimes a roommate of ours would play with him. All of my beginning tapes have him screaming in the background.

Molly: How did your friends react to you having a baby?

Mary: My friends in New Jersey were pretty good about it. Here, they were freaked out.

I've been learning about different class things. I grew up working-class and most of my friends were working-class or people of color. When I moved here all of my friends were suddenly middle-class and all alternative-y. I thought, "Holy shit, all of my friends in New Jersey are so stupid; everyone here is really positive and amazing." I mean, they all had their own businesses. Eventually, I realized that is because they were raised middle class. There are areas where they don't have that much attention for my kid. I always have these emotional breakdowns or feel really negative and they can't take it, whereas my friends back home can take it.

Molly: Yeah, that's been true for me too. One of the big arguments that people threw at me to try to convince me to have an abortion was "You don't have health insurance." It was just this strange and desperate argument because so many people don't have health insurance. Definitely middle-class people get more freaked out about babies and not having money.

As a mom, how was touring?

Mary: We went on a 10-day tour last January. It was harder than I thought it would be. Leaving Random was hard; that was the longest I ever left him. Also it's really hard to be a band touring for the first time. We played this place in LA called Club Sucker and this nine-foot-tall, black drag queen, Miss Vaginal Cream Davis, was the host. She's really funny, but she makes fun of everybody so bad. She was saying, "These bands are very white and very rich and all related to Mr. Bill Gates." It was funny but horrible and there was this huge crowd of crazy drunk people. I actually had the best time there because, again, when things are harder I usually feel like, "Fuck this, I'll teach these people a lesson." I get really fiery, so I had one of my best shows.

Molly: How has it been logistically having band practice and recording?

Mary: With my most recent band, Circles and Squares, we didn't have a place to practice since I was living in a school bus and [my bandmate] has a tiny apartment. So we played in the laundry room of her apartment building, which was really embarrassing because people would come in and be trying to do their laundry. A friend let us practice in his basement for a while, which was really nice. If I could have practiced at my house it would have been better because we could have done it while Random was sleeping. It was always a huge episode to get to where we were going to practice. When I was living in the school bus, it was easier time-wise because I'd have Random three and a half days a week and then I worked at a daycare for two days and the other day I would spend on music. Now I live in a more expensive place and I have to work more; it's harder to find time. I've been swearing I'm going to start recording on my four-track, but I just keep looking at it.

It's really hard to get focused on recording. I sit down and play little songs, and I find that I always have to have a tape recorder ready, otherwise I just forget them. I can sit down and play a little song for a while, but I can't sit down and deal with the four-track. I put out a tape about a month or two ago called *School Bus* of all the songs I had recorded in the school bus on Random's little Fisher-Price tape recorder. That was cool because it made me feel like I could still do it.

The thing that seems so hopeless to me, in terms of playing music and doing it independently, is that you hear about all of these people like Ani DiFranco who did it all on their own, but they didn't have kids. To do that, I think you have to be out there playing in all different places; I just can't do that. It's frustrating because unless you're on a major label it would be hard to make it and make any money doing music.

Molly: Before I had Hugo I didn't care about making money, but now if I am spending a lot of time and energy on something, it needs to generate some income.

Mary: You have to make the money to get by. The more time you spend making money, the less time you have for making music.

Molly: Do you hang out with other moms?

Mary: One of the hardest things as a mom is feeling isolated from other moms. For years all of my friends were from my first year in college. They didn't ever have any kids and it is really hard to have close relationships with them. Yet, I wasn't able to connect with other moms. Now it's shifting. I'm noticing who I want to be friends with, who I want to build close relationships with. There are two moms now that I am totally going after. One of them is a musician, too, and her daughter is eight. I was homeless for a while and moving from place to place and she said, "I have this school bus; if you fix it up you can take it somewhere." She was the first person who helped me in a practical way, not just [saying], "You don't have a place to live, how sad."

My other friend who's a mom was raised working-class. One of the hardest things is making friends with a mom of the same class background. She reminds me so much of myself and my mom most of the time that I just can't take it. If we can hang out without the kids it's really good so we try to do that. I want to make friends with all kinds of moms, especially moms that seem more mainstream. I think when Random starts school that will be easier because right now I just feel like a freak.

Molly: But then you'll be in the PTA. . . . Hey, have your parents heard the CD?

Mary: Actually, I think my mom hasn't listened to it—she's scared, she thinks it's all about her, and who knows? Maybe she's right. My dad, my brother, even my grandparents listened to it. They asked my dad, "Why does she have to go yelling around about that teenage welfare mother stuff?" My dad enjoyed it. I made him give me a review; for one song he said, "I don't know, this song sounds like a person who is at the end of their wits. They're not going anywhere, they're just about to fry up." Well, that probably makes sense, but for him it seems really hopeless.

Molly: It seems like more of a way of not being hopeless, like a purging thing.

Mary: Exactly.

Molly: What kind of thing will you be doing next?

Mary: I've gotten really depressed about playing shows. I'm frustrated with the music scene here. I want to focus on recording for now. I have the dream of organizing shows and having more diverse bands. I would want the show to be more of a planned event. Everyone would contribute ideas and make stuff for it. And everyone would make money based on the fact that they put this energy into creating a show. It would be about putting something forth for the audience and supporting each other in what we wanted to do and express. In my ideal world the money would be about what makes sense rather than who is popular . . .

We played Yo Yo a Go Go last summer, and our little piece of the review said, "Maybe if I were a mother I would care about the things she was singing about." I was so mad. That is just it—that is exactly the epitome of the evil. People mostly sing about the same shit, relationships or love, and you don't say, "Maybe if I were in love I would care about that."

Molly: What were your expectations of having a kid and how were they different from the reality?

Mary: I don't think I had any expectations. I was 19, I was terrified, but I couldn't get an abortion. I was raised in the Southern Baptist Church and there was all of this abortion propaganda in my face all the time. If I hadn't had all of that shit, I probably would have had an abortion, but it was too much baggage.

One thing I thought was if you just raise your kid nicely, then he'll just be nice. I thought if I did things that make sense, Random would just be good. That is definitely not the case. I didn't realize how hard it would be to have friends who aren't parents. I had no idea how hard things would be in my relationship with Random's dad. Those three things were real shockers.

Molly: The song "Heartbreak" really gets me. I had this idea that my friends and community, not to mention Hugo's dad, would want to help out and be part of raising this kid; the reality was a huge heartbreak.

Mary: When David and I were breaking up and moving apart, all of these friends said, "We want to support you," and "I'll move in with you." When it came down to it, no one was going to do it. When I moved back in with David, people thought I was being stupid, but I'm just like, "You can go live out in the desert and eat your locusts, because I've done it long enough. If I'm going to find someone who will live with me and really do it, then I'm going to do it."

Molly: I continually have this resentment or disappointment with everyone, whether they said outright they were going to support me or not, because I think that it is just not human to ignore your friends because they have a baby. It's definitely not adaptive. I actually got kicked out of my house for being pregnant.

Mary: When I was looking for a place when Random was two, no one would live with us. People aren't hateful; they are just dumb. People don't realize that children are just another aspect of diversity.

Molly: That reminds me of the song "Crashing Cars." The way I identify with the lyrics is that I am this huge disruption just for having a kid, like I am the car crash.

Mary: Totally. I've been in so many situations where all of these people who are not used to kids are there, and the kids are in the center of the room and nobody is paying attention to them. Then suddenly Random hits somebody and everyone turns and yells, "Random!" I remember once just sobbing, carrying Random home. They just don't get it that if you ignore kids long enough, that's going to happen, and then you yell at them?

Molly: And then there's the crap that gets laid on you as the mom: "Why can't you control your kid?"

Mary: We are just constantly having to educate people. Otherwise, we have to deal with their shit.

News Flash

Tinky Winky Okay in Berkeley

Berkeley, California, says Power to the Purple with a resolution backing Teletubby Tinky Winky, the children's television character Reverend Jerry Falwell has been bashing for his purse-toting subversion.

"We take umbrage at the threat to personal style and choices implicit in Mr. Falwell's designation of Tinky Winky as an inappropriate role model," the resolution says. "Long live Tinky Winky and long live freedom from self-righteousness!"

Now, we just want to know why the characters have TVs in their bellies and if *that's* okay in Berkeley "Kill Your Television" California.

10 Ways to Have Fun for Under $2: Advice from the Edge

Wendy Dutton

Why should dads and grandmas get all the glory? Just because you're poor doesn't mean you can't spoil your kids. . . .

1. The Rosebud Bath

Steal roses from your neighbor's yard and sprinkle them in the tub. If roses are unavailable, any pretty flowers will do.

2. The Psychedelic Cape

Go to your local thrift store and find one of those Day-Glo flower bathrobes from the '60s. With a little trimming and some rope, it can be quickly made into a most excellent cape.

3. Love Your Sidewalk

This is one of those cases where a sharp stick might be acceptable. That and a trash-collecting bag can turn your average Walk for Sanity into a PC cleanup adventure.

4. Club Mom

Teach your kids the joys of cranking it up. Try freeze music, follow the leader, and who-can-do-the-coolest-step.

5. Way Cool Tattoos

Let them draw all over your body, then return the favor. But note that permanent markers can get strange.

6. Rear Window

Well, we all do it, so why not do it right? Teach your kids the fine art of gathering clues, making up stories, and carrying on the legacy of Harriet the Spy.

7. The Endless Pony Ride

The next time you go to Payless and they have that damned mechanical pony out front, go for it. For $2, you could buy eight rides, which might just give you enough time to read an entire magazine article.

8. Fresher Nails

For boys and girls alike, the allure of nail polish beckons, especially if you get weird with it.

9. Make Great Art

You know that ugly wall in your place? Paint some frames on it, and let the kids fill them in. The results might even be too cool to paint over when you move.

10. Tell Your Story

On the inside of your closet, let your kids narrate the story of their childhood. Write it on the walls so future tenants know what they have to live up to.

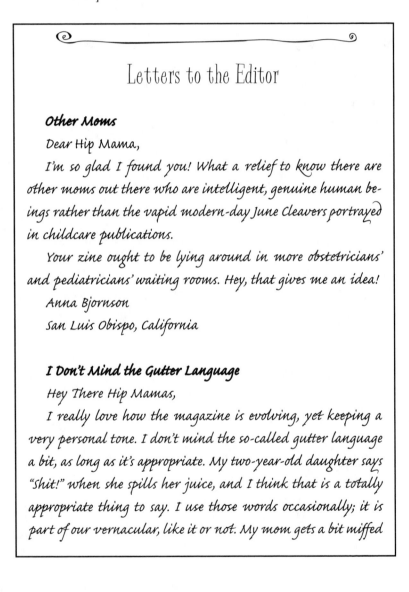

Letters to the Editor

Other Moms

Dear Hip Mama,

I'm so glad I found you! What a relief to know there are other moms out there who are intelligent, genuine human beings rather than the vapid modern-day June Cleavers portrayed in childcare publications.

Your zine ought to be lying around in more obstetricians' and pediatricians' waiting rooms. Hey, that gives me an idea!

Anna Bjornson

San Luis Obispo, California

I Don't Mind the Gutter Language

Hey There Hip Mamas,

I really love how the magazine is evolving, yet keeping a very personal tone. I don't mind the so-called gutter language a bit, as long as it's appropriate. My two-year-old daughter says "shit!" when she spills her juice, and I think that is a totally appropriate thing to say. I use those words occasionally; it is part of our vernacular, like it or not. My mom gets a bit miffed and tries to get her to say other silly things like "dagnabit," but, thankfully, it hasn't caught on yet.

Beth Karow

Soquel, California

Full Plate Living

Dear Hip Mama,

It's around 2 A.M. (everyone is asleep finally) and I'm finally writing this "Thank You" for your fabulous zine and The Hip Mama Survival Guide. I've composed several letters and conversations with you in my head as I rock, nurse, read to, sing to, and clean up after my 21-month-old and 3-month-old babies. It's also winter and I'm probably in the throes of MAJOR CABIN FEVER! (I'm in Chicago and we've got about three feet of snow.) Anyway, your zine is so cool—totally talks about what I want to know, makes me feel like "I'm not the only one. . . ." And thanks to your book, I picked up C. P. Estes's Women Who Run with the Wolves and am loving that, too. Between all this great reading, my son, Remi, and daughter, Raven, this spring (hopefully) school, and sometimes a part-time job, I've got a totally full plate—I know every mom does.

Your zine inspires me to get back on track and do my thing, make my art. It also validates the feeling that there is TOTAL CREATIVITY and artistry in raising children—they're a major contribution to this society (at least that's the goal, right?). Anyway, I'm a sculptor/painter, freelance photographer, ex-sex worker (dominatrix, go-go dancer at my fave dyke bars, performance artist), and art college dropout. One big dream, I guess, is to somehow contribute to your zine that I love so much. Enough talking, thanks and keep up that great work!

Joanne Vargas-Vales

Oak Park, Illinois

Transitions

Sunday	Monday	Tuesday	Wednesday
		1 On way to park, eight-year-old sez: "Mom, no one knows how weird you are."	**2** Homeschooling co-op falls apart. Visit a dozen private schools.
6 Relax w/ kids at lake. Feel old when I call 21-year-old lifeguard "the kid."	**7** Have Dad take us to fancy French restaurant. Kid orders fries.	**8** On street Dad sez: "Millions and millions of years of evolution . . . for this?"	**9** Decide it's zine's fault, therefore your fault, that I'm going blind.
13 Stay up all night with jet lag & "I have no kid with me" fever. Sleep til 2 P.M.	**14** Get tattoo. Party with radical mamas. Geek out when they call me "the kid."	**15** Stay up all night with high school boyfriend. Keep forgetting I'm not 16.	**16** Fly home on same dreaded airline. Flight attendants tell folk to "shut up."
20 Is this art imitating life or the other way around?	**21** Work for 24 hours on zine, then start on final draft of book proposal.	**22** Play Monopoly with kids. Lose. Accept that I will always be on welfare.	**23** Bleach parts of hair & dye purple to hide grey.
27 Road trip! Small town stares. Kid sez: *They* know how weird you are."	**28** Wake up on High Sierra mountain to see sunrise. Drive home.	**29** Cancel therapy. Become fascinated with the Olsen twins.	**30** Finish off Rocket Espresso. Work all night on zine.

Thursday	Friday	Saturday
3 Take kids to Grandma's house for chicken-naming ceremony.	**4** Grandpa shows up with electronic pets for kids. Most die by evening.	**5** OD on Rocket Espresso. Try to do month's worth of work in 24 hours.
10 Hate mail sez: "Breeder loser! I can't believe you do a zine for breeder losers!"	**11** Fly all night to NYC on discount airline. Plane sounds like a VW.	**12** Meet with editor after sleeping two hours in a doorway.
17 Radio host calls & sez: "We're in the middle of a teen mom debate. Talk!"	**18** Field calls from people who say I sounded half asleep & lame on the radio.	**19** Sit around waiting for email. Contemplate clit piercing.
24 Kid begs to go to Roswell, New Mexico, to see aliens. Take her to see clowns instead.	**25** New mom moves in nearby. Imagine mama neighborhood takeover.	**26** Buy couch too big for door. Recruit mamas to hoist it up over balcony.
31 Hard drive crashes. Seriously consider getting real job.		

yo mama's daybook

Pregnant Again

Susan Ito

It's like This. Your house is a mess.
Socks under The coffee Table,
congealing dishes sTacked on The microwave.
A whining, like a power drill in your ear:
Gummy bears, I wanT guuuummmmmy bears!
EighT-page Term paper due Tomorrow.
Sick To your sTomach, you wake up aT Three,
sweaTy, having To pee.
You don'T have a clue whaT's going on.
The doorbell rings. IT's company. You are
dressed in pajamas.
IT's seven in The morning. You sTand wiTh your back
To The door, breaThing quieTly, hoping They will give up
and go away. They ring The bell again.
Who is IT? Then, before you even look Through The
Tiny peephole, you know. IT's Second Child.
WaiT. You run To The calendar. WaiT. You yell

Through the window, you weren't supposed to come
until next year. You wave your watch in the air.
NEXT YEAR. Read my lips.
Second Child is patient, cheerful. Helps self to milk
in the refrigerator, gulping right from the bottle.
Nice place you have here.
Place, yes the place is fine, but the time,
the time you see
is all wrong. Listen, it's lovely to see you, but
I need to tell you. I'm in graduate school.
This isn't going to work.
Graduate school? Wonderful, says Second Child.
I'll help you write. I love the sound of typing, it
puts me right to sleep. BUT . . .
You sneak a glance at First Child. She is
rocking a stuffed armadillo to sleep, kisses it
on the nose. Babies are sweet, she says.
You want to know how much Second Child paid her
to say that. A year's worth of gummy bears.
You wave your hand in front of its face.
You're not real, you say. Give me a sign. Prove it.
Gritting your teeth, you pee according to
the instructions on the box. The test strip
turns a brilliant, unmistakable pink.
Second Child, a showoff, is laughing. When you order
that cap and gown . . . ask for size XXXL. Big enough for
both of us.

I Don't Wanna Be a Mother Anymore!

Opal Palmer Adisa

I am certain I am the only mother who sometimes feels as if she doesn't want to do this anymore, that she can't do this anymore, that no matter what she does she is wrong.

I am certain I am the only mother who fears she will be accused of being unfit in more ways than she can figure out. I am certain I am the only mother who just doesn't see any way out of failing, that I'm the only mother who feels it's near impossible to be a sometimes-okay mother to three children with their own individual personalities and myriad demands.

This has been a particularly difficult week for me, and consequently for my children. I am not sure why it has been so hard. I am sure that PMS blues and then four agonizing days of menstrual cramps didn't help. I am sure having two essays and a curriculum to write and not making any headway with any of them didn't help. I am sure feeling exhausted and wanting someone there to hold me tight didn't help. I am sure just worrying about the mounting bills, the things I want to accomplish in my life, what I want for each of my children, and how to raise them to be positive, productive adults didn't help. I am certain I am the

97

only mother who trips herself up worrying how best to help her children realize their dreams, and I am sure my constant worrying didn't help. I am certain that life didn't help, especially since time was wearing Rollerblades, speeding around on skates, and time being against me didn't help. I am certain that yearning for a quiet spot with warm water lapping at the shore and the sun's rays radiating my body didn't help. Instead I had the life I had and I had the three children I had and they had me, and that certainly didn't help at all!

There is nothing worse than sending my kids to bed and not being able to find a dark spot to cry in because I am aching so much from observing how difficult it must be to live with me. Nothing worse than realizing that I don't know how—or am unable—to pull back once I am in the midst of the situation. Then when I finally get a moment, I feel so bad from aching about the scars I am inflicting. And there is no place to cry . . . the tears won't come because I can't do anything about who I am, what I demand of myself and my children, and how they respond to my rule, and conversely, how I react to their defiance. They are always defiant.

I know I am not the parent my children need. I told my son that I love him, but I am not the mother he needs or maybe even deserves, because I don't know how to mother him. I must confess I don't want the work of mothering anymore. I don't want to give the energy it requires. I feel too close to my children. I want too much for them, want to guide them to achieve what they want for themselves. I want them to be successful yet compassionate. I want them to be articulate leaders, and yet be concerned with and committed to the community. I want them to pursue their dreams but not be selfish. I want them to understand that the world is bigger than where they live and what they can imagine. I want them to live life with vigor, to be bold, to be happy, to always search for the truth. I don't want them to be afraid to fail and try again. I want them to do their best at all times. I don't want them to acquiesce to authority. I want them to love me just one-tenth as much as I love them. I want them to have a future. I don't want to damage them.

Every moment of my waking day and even sleeping night I am pre-occupied with them, praying for their safety, constantly analyzing how I behave toward them and what kind of behavior I am modeling and the negative impact that I might have on them because I resent them. I resent them requiring so much of me. I resent the time I have to spend caring for them. I resent that I want so much for them. I resent that I worry so much about them. I resent the responsibility of being their mother. I resent the fact that I can't help but look at them and think, *Gosh, they are really gorgeous human beings,* and feel myself go soft every time. I resent the deep passion they pull from me so noncha-lantly. That's why I want to abandon my role, to give them away and free myself of their weight.

I know I am the only mother who loves her children but doesn't want to cope with them daily. I know I am the only mother who feels burdened by the nuclear family lifestyle. I know I am the only mother who is certain that she is messing up royally but doesn't know how to stop or fix the situation. This week has been a week from hell and I wish neither my children nor I had been present for it, but we were. I would like to blame my anemia and menses for conspiring against me but it would sound too much like the very thing I accuse my children of: not wanting to take responsibility for their own actions.

How do you teach without lecturing?

How do you teach without criticizing?

Is it really, as my teenage daughter says, me making too much of her burning the cabbage while standing in the kitchen with the telephone glued to her ear? And why am I so irked by her constant chatter? Do I fear she will become a gossiping adult? What do I see in my son's burst of anger that ignites and matches my own tendency toward inflammation? And what about the blind stubbornness of my youngest that sometimes makes me want to lock her out of the house? Most times I think I am too easygoing, that I let them get away with murder, as the saying goes. So sometimes, like this week, I put my foot down and it is too heavy. Everyone, including myself, is bruised by it. I don't like myself as a strict, nonbudging mother, but sometimes I just need—would like—for my children to do what I say the first time I say it, without fussing or arguing or interrogating my every motive.

Sorry, it's not up for discussion today. Just do it because I said so. Don't you just hate the person who says that until you realize it is you saying that, and then you kind of respect the you standing up for yourself against your three children?

I'm sure I am the only mother who is seeking a happy medium and who feels certain that it doesn't exist. What I really want to do is run away. I want to run as far away as I can and not look back. I understand now the fear and frustration of those mothers who left and never looked back. Then I wouldn't have to worry about how I am failing or not failing my children, the people I love most and for whom I want only the best.

My children deserve a nicer mother, one who is not so demanding, so stressed, so exacting, so critical, and so tyrannical. I am hearing myself say, more and more, "Because I say so!" I hate those four words but I say them anyway because I just don't have the energy or patience to justify myself to three inquiring children today. *Excuse me, but I am not your debate partner today.* I hear myself screaming and I hate the person who is screaming like an out-of-control crazy woman, which I am, but I can't stop myself. I hear a woman going on and on, knowing she should stop, that she has already made her point, but she continues, and I cringe realizing it is me. Then I shut up and don't respond to them because I don't want to say the wrong thing or go off again, and my silence makes them feel shitty and I feel even shittier knowing they are feeling shitty trying to gauge my silence.

I know I am the only mother who sometimes takes to bed to nurse her tears, crying over how poorly she is mothering. I know I am the only mother who wishes she could stop herself before she goes too far. I know I am the only mother my children have, and I know I am not always the best person for them to be around. And what I really want is to be a good mother to each of my children every day. So here are 12 things I should have said to them last week but was unable to . . .

12 Things Every Mother Should Tell Their Children

1. I love you and I am not perfect.
2. I love you and you are not perfect, either.
3. I love you and I am doing the best I can.
4. I love you and you must never allow me or anyone else to cripple or impede who you are.
5. I love you and you have a right to receive love and praise daily.
6. I love you and sometimes I just need you to do what I asked because I asked.
7. I love you and forgive me for all my errors.
8. I love you and never let me or anyone else stop you from being the best.
9. I love you because you are unique.

10. I love you and want all the good things in life for you.
11. I love you and I am just trying to guide you into a safe and happy adulthood.
12. I love you and never let my failings or shortcomings dictate the rest of your life.

Widows I Have Known

Miriam Sagan

When I was widowed at the age of 41, I made a list of widows so I wouldn't feel so anomalous.

Yoko Ono
Courtney Love
Patti Smith
Madame Max
Wife of Bath
Fermina Daza
Coretta Scott King
Cousin Becky
Jackie Kennedy
Elizabeth Taylor
Mary Shelley
Kate Chopin

Cousin Becky

I remember when my cousin Joe died and left his wife, Becky, a widow.

I must have been about 10 years old. It was just around the time that the Surgeon General's report came out on cigarettes and lung cancer, and, as if on cue, Joe got a terrible pain in his back that turned out to be a tumor, and he died.

Joe was a notoriously unfaithful husband. His famous remark, which my father once repeated to me after two beers, was, "It's not infidelity if you can't get it at home." My brother and I spent many hours laughing over this and trying to figure out exactly what Joe couldn't get, but of course at that time it was serious family business. Joe had a mistress in Manhattan, and my grandfather, his boss, advised Becky to start driving in from Long Island against traffic to pick Joe up every evening at six o'clock sharp.

Apparently the problem had started on their honeymoon. My father knew this because he had been on that honeymoon. It was the height of the Great Depression, and as a treat my grandmother drove Joe and Becky down to Florida. My father and his younger brother came along.

Joe died. My cousin Becky became what I knew of widows. She was 42 and a grandmother. Her greatest goal in life was to keep her kitchen floor clean. I once dropped a spotless apple on her spotless floor and she tried to throw it out. My mother, who couldn't bear to waste food, intervened and let me eat it.

New Jersey Widow

I am 42 years old. I live with my parents and my young daughter in the New Jersey house I grew up in. Every morning I put on my tight black suit and go to work as a bookkeeper for my father's cousin. My father's cousin runs a notoriously corrupt trucking company. I walk into my office, take off my suit jacket, and hang it on the back of the chair so it won't get wrinkled. I arrive at 8:15 A.M. and leave by 3:20 P.M. so I can pick up my daughter from school. She comes running down the hill with her pink lunch box. We go home to my parents' quiet house. My father is retired and he breeds rare orchids. My mother still works in a tailoring shop.

Every Friday and Saturday night, I go out with a different man. I am set up constantly by my cousins, my boss, the foreman at work, people I went to high school with. I let these men take me to nice family-style Italian restaurants, Jewish delis, and Greek diners. We go to the movies or dancing in a club. We would no sooner venture into Manhattan than go to the moon.

The problem is, I start to lie. I say my husband drowned racing a yacht across the Atlantic. I say he died of AIDS-like symptoms that probably weren't AIDS. I say I loved him so passionately that I threw myself into the open grave. They do not ask me out a second time. They are heavyset New Jersey men in their 40s or 50s. Some wear gold pinkie rings. Some are divorced. There seems to be an endless supply of them. On Sunday nights, I stay home.

On the Border

Ana Consuela made me laugh at my own husband's funeral. She told me a story about her aunt on the border. Her aunt was about 40 when her husband died. He was a lawyer who owned some buildings; he left the aunt some money. After his death, she visited his grave each Sunday. Ana's mother would drive the aunt to the cemetery. The aunt wore her black lace mantilla over the long black hair that all the tall Sonoran women in Ana's family boasted. Her wrists smelled like the rose water she dabbed from a blue cobalt bottle the exact shade of the desert sky turning from blue to night at 5:45 on a winter's afternoon in Nogales. She dabbed rose water behind her pretty ears and on her ample cleavage, and then she threw herself down on the grave. Ana's mother could hear everything she said. The aunt would pray violently, cross herself, and fall to her knees. Her mantilla would swing like a curtain between the worlds.

She'd say, "You son of a bitch, while you were alive I never prospered. Why did you let those rents go? Do you have any idea what that property is worth? Well, listen . . ." She'd recite, like she was reading from a ledger book, in dollars and pesos, what she was getting for each property. What she had bought and what she sold. Securities, silver, bonds. She listed her worth to her worthless dead husband.

Ana Consuela made me laugh. She threw herself down on the ground, imitating her aunt.

"Did she remarry?" I wanted to know.

"No, she just made money. Died a rich woman," Ana said.

Sharon made me laugh at my husband's funeral, too. She sidled up to me as I sat stunned and weeping and she hissed in my ear, "My great aunt Tilly in Brooklyn was widowed when she was 78 and was remarried in a scandalous seven months."

Sharon's voice was breathy and confiding. It tickled my ears, as did her red curls. About 45 minutes later she cozied up to me again: "My cousin Irma was 91 when she was widowed and she was remarried in five months!"

Later I asked Sharon if this was true, and she stood by her story. I could see her relatives, tiny Russian Jewish ladies smelling of rose water in dark New York apartments with lace doillies and potted geraniums. Like Sharon, they always managed to have a husband, until their own deaths parted them from number three or four.

I liked these Mexican and Jewish widows. They smelled of rose water. They smelled of change.

So You're Trying for the Girl???

Kathryn Reiss

When word of my third pregnancy started making the rounds, my phone rang a lot more often than it usually does. Friends and neighbors called to offer congratulations and to inquire about my health—and invariably asked, "A third child? You must be trying for a girl!" Sometimes they phrased it slightly differently: "Maybe this time it will be a girl," or "I bet you're hoping for a girl," or "Don't worry, sooner or later you'll get a girl," or "Third time's the charm."

Some friends recommended special tests to divine the baby's sex: "Hang your wedding ring over your belly on a string and watch. . . . If it moves in a straight line back and forth, it's a boy. If it turns in a circle, it's a girl." "Go out of the room and have someone hide a knife and a pair of scissors under the couch while you're gone. Then come in and sit down—and if you sit on the cushion with the knife underneath, it's a boy. But if you sit on the cushion with the scissors underneath, it's a girl!"

I guess it goes without saying that my husband and I already have two boys. They are 10 and 5 years old, and light up our lives with their presence. We wouldn't trade them for girls, not ever. And so all the enthusiastic responses from my friends got on my nerves. "What's the big deal about girls?" I'd mutter under my breath. I mean, sure I'd be happy to have a girl, it would be a change, and a chance for me to indulge myself by buying all those adorable dresses and things until she grew old enough to stop me. I would be delighted to have a girl for my third child. But the fact is, I would be delighted to have a boy for my third child, too. The fact is, I want three children or more.

And that, I've come to realize, is what people are really talking about. It's not about girls or boys, it's about the decision to have a third child at all. The idea of any family choosing to have more than two children stops a lot of people in their tracks.

Think about it. Society always takes an interest in our reproductive plans. The newly married couple gets it from their parents and friends as soon as they return from their Hawaiian honeymoon: "So, when will we be hearing the pitter-pat of little feet?" or "We're so excited about becoming grandparents!" or "You two don't want to wait too long now. . . ."

After the first child is born, the public scrutiny doesn't let up: "You don't want him to grow up an only child, do you?" or "Only children have such hard lives!" or "Don't you think it's about time to start trying for a little brother or sister for Baby?" It is natural, people assume, that a family will not be complete until it has two children. Best arrangement is one boy and one girl, but two—of either sex—will do. And once the two children are born, the public is appeased. The parents have done what is expected of them. They have produced replacements for themselves on the planet and they have produced a necessary sibling for each child's social and emotional development. Each parent can carry a child in the baby seat of a bicycle and look after a child in a restaurant. One parent can hold two children's hands crossing the street. Daycare costs are possible to meet. College educations can be saved for. Parents can rent a two-bedroom apartment without feeling crowded. The whole family can fit in small cars, sleep in four-person tents, stay in a standard room in motels, and go on trips to visit relatives without overwhelming their hosts.

The public eye closes.

But it pops open again when a third pregnancy is announced.

Three children are so much more than two, somehow. In our society, having three children is not environmentally sound; it does not control population growth; it may bespeak ignorance or foolishness on the part of careless parents. In any case, an explanation seems to be called for.

And so we get the knowing smiles. "Sooo, you must be hoping for a girl this time!" goes a long way to explain why a couple would go beyond two—and it's a lot kinder than, "Uh-oh! Weren't you on the pill?" or "*Another baby? Your biological clock must have been ticking pretty loudly . . .*"

I get the feeling that no one quite believes me when I tell them I always wanted to have a lot of children. I mean, a whole lot. Six or 10 or 12. My favorite books when I was a kid were about big families, with children scrambling pell-mell around the house, with parents mixing up names, with sets of twins and triplets complicating things, with houses bursting at the seams. Friends who grew up in large families tend to roll their eyes at me and tell me I'm buying the fantasy—that real life in large families was tough, that there wasn't enough parental time or attention or money to go around, that brothers and sisters were bullies. They tell me I had a lucky escape.

I didn't buy it then, nor do I now.

Only a generation ago, families with five or more children were commonplace. It was the time of the Brady Bunch, the Partridge Family, the Jackson Five, the Osmonds. You didn't have to be Catholic to explain being part of a crowd. In the neighborhood where I grew up in Ohio, there were families with six kids, with eight, scads with five. Three or four kids was just normal. Two was small. One was downright pitiful.

A girl in my class was one of 10—I remember going to play at her house after school and watching, awed, while she made us a snack. There were two refrigerators in the kitchen! And two stoves! The bedrooms were set up like dormitories, with clusters of bunk beds and rows of dressers. How could my own boring kitchen with its single fridge and stove measure up? Or my bedroom, with the canopy bed, shared with no one?

I tried to convince my parents I needed to be one of a pack. I wanted to have siblings galore. I would take care of all of them, I promised. I would be the best big sister ever. We might even form our own rock group.

"Go get some baby-sitting jobs," they advised.

Eventually I realized I would have to create my own pack.

Economics being what they are today, however, not to mention my husband being what he is, the baker's dozen of babies I once envisioned has shrunk to a more manageable trio. But three today still feels like a pack—confirmed by the wide, disbelieving eyes of friends and acquaintances on hearing the news of this third, outrageous pregnancy.

So, no, we weren't trying for the girl. We were just trying for yet another baby. I don't need to spin my ring or check for hidden scissors; I know that what we get will be exactly what I've wanted all along.

News Flash

Barbie Gets a Makeover

In 1998, Barbie got a makeover. Formerly with measurements equivalent to 38"-18"-34", Barbie got a smaller chest and hips, and a wider waist. She also got brownish hair—as opposed to bleach-blond or jet black—and flat feet. But while Barbie may have evolved to stand on her own two feet without falling over, she certainly wouldn't be speaking for herself any time soon. Her once-toothy glamour girl grin was turned into a very demure, close-mouthed smile.

Mattel Toys was supposedly succumbing to a demand from its target market—girls aged 3 to 11—to make Barbie "cooler." Sean Fitzgerald, vice president of corporate communications for Mattel, said, "They wanted Barbie to be more reflective of themselves."

Which makes us wonder: Does Barbie really reflect little girls' desires? Or merely the male toy designers' own plastic desires?

Weaning Sucks

Keely Eastley

here is a piece missing in the literature about extended breast-feeding: The voice of a woman who has nursed well beyond the first year, whose child hasn't naturally decreased nursing or "weaned himself," and who is reaching her limit.

Recently, my two-year-old son, Nicky, and I went through the process of weaning. Because I had always planned for him to wean himself, it stirred up feelings of anger, failure, and grief in me, but all of this was followed by a slow-growing appreciation of the new place we had arrived at together.

In Nicky's infancy, it was important to me to be child-centered. From the day he was born at home, he has shared the family bed and was breastfed solely on demand. But as he became a toddler, we began to feel an imbalance in the household. At 18 months, Nicky was still nursing at least eight times during the day, not counting all of his jumping down and scrambling back into my lap moments later; his night nursing was still usually about every two hours. My husband, Nate, and I were almost totally neglecting our own needs in our gusto to meet Nicky's. What little intimacy we were able to squeeze in was dwindling, and we noticed the beginnings of a wedge.

I became angry and resentful about the amount of nursing Nicky was doing and about my frequently interrupted sleep. His gymnastics and yanking at my shirt and bra and his urge to fondle my other breast were extremely tiresome. I needed to have some say in our nursing relationship; I needed to establish some limits.

First, I decided not to nurse in public anymore. Later, I stopped nursing him while eating or sitting on the toilet. Then, I established a certain place in the house for nursing. Surprisingly, Nicky was quick to learn and adapt to the new guidelines.

It dawned on me that I had begun to wean him. Gently and gradually, but I had begun the process all the same.

With each step, I found a sea of calm, only to be followed by a tempest of angry feelings and resentment. I wanted to push him off my body. There were times I had to leave the room to release this inner pressure. Sometimes I didn't make it out before growling and throwing a pillow or hitting the bed. I kept searching my heart for a possible next step that would work for both Nicky and myself.

As I struggled with these feelings, I talked to other nursing moms, former nursing moms, and La Leche League leaders. I read parenting books, spoke to my midwife, and did whatever I could for support. My question turned out to be "How do you wean?"

Basically two scenarios emerged—go cold turkey or let the child lead the weaning, which could mean nursing until age four or older. Both options filled me with despair. I simply couldn't cut Nicky off, but the possibility of nursing for two more years was beyond anything I could imagine. I felt trapped.

The more impatient I was with Nicky, the more he wanted to nurse. We both got short-tempered and cranky.

One weekend when Nate was away, Nicky was having a hard time sleeping and was nursing every hour and a half. At 4 A.M. he started grabbing at my other breast. I removed his hand as I always did, and he began to wail. I tried to get him to nurse, but he was too angry and frustrated. All he could do was cry. I snapped and screamed, "What do you want? You cry if you nurse, you cry if you don't nurse. I can't win. You're driving me crazy. Now lie down and go to sleep."

He was so scared, he put his head on the pillow and quickly closed his eyes.

I looked down at my boy and became deeply afraid. I thought of my own childhood, how long-lasting the wounds from words can be. Something inside me told me I was in a dangerous place and needed to stop nursing. I had reached my limit, and a meanness was beginning to steal its way out. I thought, I just have to get through the first 24 hours, then I'll be able to do it.

We went all day the next day without nursing. By this time, Nicky was used to nursing first thing in the morning, then again midafternoon. By 5 P.M. he was crying and upset. I held him and kept explaining, "Mommy will hold and comfort you, but we aren't going to nurse anymore."

When Nate walked in the door I felt relief, and my resolve began to crumble. He would support whatever I felt I needed to do. That's all he could do. But I wanted him to be the one to say, "Yes, you must do this," or "No, you must nurse him."

I swept Nicky into my arms and sat in our spot and nursed him. I felt everything go to peace. Nicky was instantly at ease. It was how we had been from the moment he was born. I nursed him all that night.

The next morning I awoke from this dream: I am riding on the subway; I look up and realize I have missed my stop and must go back.

It didn't take me long to figure out that I needed to complete what I had started the day before. I was fooling myself if I thought I wouldn't meet the same fierce anger again, and I was afraid Nicky would meet it, too.

Part of me just wanted to escape and resume nursing. I was running from the discomfort and the pain of my own truth. That afternoon, I talked it over with Nate and decided what I already knew in my heart. We went all that day and night without nursing. Nicky cried, and I held him and soothed him. I cried, too. The first day was the most difficult.

The following day, Nicky was unexpectedly cheery, and that second night, he slept five hours before waking up. He had moments of frustration and anger, but within three days, he no longer asked for the breast. It took the push and pull out of our relationship, and I think he was relieved.

It left me feeling sad. Nursing was a way of being with my son I wouldn't have anymore. My body missed it all the way to my womb. Yet, to continue would have been impossible.

I felt I had failed. I had wanted to nurse until Nicky decided to stop. All the parenting I had done up to this point was part of that philosophy. I kept thinking that if it hadn't been for my personal defect, I could still be nursing. But I was trapped by my own ideology. Parenting is a flowing, ever-changing relationship, not a static philosophy.

I had to honor my limits in order to be truly loving. I was tolerating nursing, not loving while nursing. After three months, I had finally completed the weaning process, and I am loving my son the best way I know how—by loving myself.

The Other Day When I Was Poor

Maia Swift, age 7

The other day when I was poor
(And listen to this, chicks out there
I know it sounds silly
But really . . .)

The other day when I went to school
I was up on the high bar structure
And that boy pushed me off it
And I lost three back teeth

And the next week
I was up on the highest bars
And he pulled me off them

But when I got home
I put those teeth under my pillow
And got $100 from the tooth fairy
Wasn't poor no more

117

GRUNGE BOY

IN PRE-SCHOOL
THEY CALLED
HIM THE
HAND-ME-DOWN
CHILD, BUT
DUE TO A
STRANGE
TWIST IN
FASHION HE
ENTERED
KINDERGARTEN
THE HIPPEST
KID IN THE
CLASS...

Been Around the Block

Bill Donahue

For most of July, the boundary was the edge of the yard. Allie, my 13-month-old daughter, could play in the grass and the trickle of hose water that we ran sometimes on the marigolds. But if she toddled past the driveway, we grabbed her and she arched her back, screaming. Allie had watched both of us, her mother and I, venture past the corner—seen us disappear like ships off the edge of the world, and now she wanted to know what was Out There.

Our city block is on a fairly steep hill. Earthquakes and frost heaves have ripped cracks in the pavement and skateboarders slalom among kids on bikes. I was afraid it was not a place for a baby, but my worries ultimately amounted to nothing. One night Allie elbowed me in the ribs, hard.

We were going down Alder Street first: past the Dalmatian who churns inside his fence, past the vegetable patch on the corner, and—what was this?—on toward a telephone pole with a long wire anchoring it to the ground. Allie batted the wire so it sang like a guitar, then scrambled back toward the vegetables and picked at the lettuce.

I'd seen this routine before, of course. As a parent, you can get used to the sputtering chaos and you try as best you can to go forward:

Get out of the grocery store before your kid sees the candy. Get out of the lettuce before your neighbor shows up with an admonishing scowl. I reached for Allie now but she wobbled past me, her tiny legs jerking like a new marionette. She stepped onto the pavement, then abruptly she crashed. There was blood on her knee.

She shrieked; I held her. I patted the soft blond down on her head, but still she sobbed on, twisting and raucously kicking until finally I just set her down. I had to.

And now there were baby carriages on the street, and cats that had come out in the cool of the evening to slink through the grass. Allie chased after a marmalade kitten, then stumbled upon two plastic flamingos which, valiantly, she tried to pry free.

It was absurd. Usually, it took me less than three minutes to reach these flamingos; Allie and I had been out for nearly an hour. All that kept me going was this: Somehow, miraculously, we were making our way around the block. We were closing in on the third corner. My kid was going to pull this one off.

We kept going—past the house with the mossy rocks in the yard, then over a metal grate that clanged wonderfully when you leapt on it. At the last corner, there were pinecones. Allie grabbed one; squealing, she pushed it up to my hip. I laughed, but then she flailed her arms at me, grunting. No words (she couldn't talk then), but still she reminded me of a hike I took once—of the way the trail cut through a rock tunnel under a waterfall. You could stand inside the tunnel and feel the rock shake. That surprised me, and now Allie was surprised by this pinecone. It was new to her, and she was scraping it on my leg. "Wake up, Pop," she was saying. "The world is a luminous thing."

I took that bristly pinecone—and the next one Allie handed me, and the next one, until my arms filled and I started using my pockets and Allie spun off and I had to drop the cones on the sidewalk. We went home (yes, all the way around the block), and Allie climbed into her crib and then I just stood over her. I watched as, like a wild animal after a feast, she fell quickly asleep.

News Flash

Grandmother of 15 Gives Birth to Triplets

Congratulations to Arcelia Garcia! The 54-year-old mother of eight and grandmother of 15 gave birth to triplets January 8, 2000. The healthy girls, who are not identical, were born by C-section at Yakima Valley Memorial Hospital in Washington State.

"It went very smoothly. Everything went as planned," said Francisco Garcia, Arcelia's 34-year-old son. Arcelia plans to return to work as a farmworker as soon as her health and the babies allow.

Originally from Michoacán, Mexico, Arcelia and her family moved to Washington in 1976. Her eight other children were at the hospital with her.

Giving birth to triplets in one's 50s is extremely rare, especially without fertility drugs—but Arcelia didn't need 'em. Go, mama!

Turning

Annaliese Jakimides

I made my daughter cry today. My words ripped harsh and unsympathetic: "How could you have turned down a job? You have 15 cents! And you need $2,000 for college by the 15th or you can't go. What do you mean 'the job wasn't right'?"

Silence.

"Any job would be right just about now."

The telephone rattled empty in my ear; the sound of her swallowing tears 200 miles away, our last communication. I heard my words as if through some otherworldly gauze, as if thrown from some other woman's mouth.

I am afraid. I don't know how to do this redefined mothering thing. All of my training has been in the up-close, in-your-face type of mothering, not this long-distance kind.

If someone were to ask me what I am skilled in, I would say mothering (not parenting, but mothering—which requires a mythical umbilical cord pulsing blood and pain and celebration between two bodies). I would say that. Shout it. Know it.

Damn. I've always been able to do all of these things. Say the right thing, pass no judgment, and trust that everything would be all right when she forged notes in third grade; when a five-year-old, golden-haired California girl taught her and her brother how to have a child's idea of intercourse in that gentle summer field of goldenrod and broken dandelion leaves; when a boy she adored told her that Jesus told him that she wasn't the right one for him and he was sorry, so very sorry that he had fingered the stiff nipple of her left breast.

I never knew what to do. I never knew what not to do. I just did it. Now I feel suspended, my reasoning levitating an inch above the earth, my logic hyperventilating and trying to catch its natural rhythm.

I had not realized how much I needed the physical in which to ground myself. I do not have her eyes, black as wet soil, in which to look; there is no flint of dark cheek skin from which to detect even the slightest quiver.

Dianne Benedict writes, "The feminine, in remaining attached to the child of her own shaping, consigns herself to sharing its fate and to sharing her fate with it."

I cannot share too many fates, for my umbilical cord has not yet learned to pulse with a child who has moved away, a child who is trying to learn independence firmly and wildly and joyfully, a child who has no summer job, a child who tells me not to worry, a child who has 15 cents.

Now, there have been days when I had only 15 cents. A number of them. The difference rests here: I was not my child. And here: I never told my mother.

I never told my mother about Paul Young's intense kisses either, wet on the back of my neck, and how I heard years later that he was gay and killed his funeral-director lover to inherit the business.

I never told her that Ronnie Addison and I made exquisitely nasty love in his musty basement apartment two blocks away while his six Doberman pinschers guarded the 144 rifles under our pulsing bed.

I never told her that I could have shot smack, snorted coke, done dollies and 'ludes, and quickened and flattened and soared on chemical ribbons.

Perhaps my mother was right. Maybe ignorance is bliss. Perhaps I would be better off if I did not know when my daughter made love for the first time. Perhaps I'd be better off if I did not know that he'd used her, and she him, and that they both cried. Perhaps I'd be better off not knowing that she has sipped whiskey, smoked two cigarettes, and tried marijuana (and liked the way her body floated in a world bereft of harsh angles).

But I could not stand that kind of bliss, bliss from ignorance, for my world would have no trust. Trust. I believe that's what the core of mothering is intended to be. To know my daughter down to her deepest darkness and love her anyway.

I must trust myself, too. Trust that when I reviewed the checklist for departure—beyond the T-shirts, the soap, the plastic disposable razors she insists on using—I did not overlook the basics.

She can wash her own clothes, by hand or machine—even by pumping five-gallon buckets of water from a red Deming hand pump; read labels; iron a smooth collar if she so chooses; know the shrouds under which sugar hides—dextrose, sucrose, cane, beet; judge the nutritional quality of béchamel sauce against curried lima beans; recognize the proper lay of forks on cloth napkins.

She knows about condoms and HIV and chlamydia and happy tongues. She knows about the resumption of breath and the peace of flesh against flesh. She knows how to pronounce *clitoris* and *labia*, but she still hates the sound of the word *vagina*.

She knows that dried flowers and Nana's wind-up Santas from 1944 (now ours) accumulate the dust of a dirt road in humid summer like black flies on oiled skin; that all homes, unlike houses, should smell of books handled many times by many hands; that any green oasis will soothe the raw edges of a wounded day.

She knows how to check the oil in the pickup, gas up the chainsaw and rip that honey into a deafening hum. She knows about nuclear reactors and rods and half-lives and fission and fusion and the fallacy of containment.

She knows as much as I can teach her right now without stripping myself and cheating her. The reality is, I must finally admit I cannot contain her anymore. I cannot protect her. It is a done deal. I have given her my hints and shortcuts and insights and all the skills I know how to communicate about finding answers for herself. She is smarter than I was, and I was smart for 1966, but I guess it can't ever be enough. It shouldn't be. She needs her own wounds. She needs her own stories, so many she doesn't have the time to share them with me, nor, if I am honest, the inclination.

This is the part of the job description I never realized would be the most difficult—to make myself fearlessly obsolete; to trust this sharp, irreplaceable woman, unrestrained as she has always been; to watch the first hesitant strokes of her winging into open air, and then turn.

Another Train
(Uncertain Destinations)

June Day

When I found myself dissatisfied, I did what I had always done. I got on the train. I got on the train for an indefinite period with an uncertain destination to ride my blues away. I looked out the splashed and scratched window, watching trees clustered like gentlemen, scattered porches, puddles, purebred ponies, Pekinese, urban and suburban sprawl, looking for a sign. I would know, like lightning, like a slap, like ascension: "This is it." And then I'd emerge from the belly of the train, pure and good and ready for my true destiny. Or, I mean, "we." That was the difference, the changed variable, the infant daughter. There were more changed variables: the car seat, the whining, the stroller; things that demanded coordination, skill in handling, and, moreover, planning.

But into the iron horse we climbed, like Trojan soldiers, and were carried. I fed my tiny family with daily miracles, turning water into milk. And we passed from one sea to Minneapolis to Spokane to another sea, on a strange tour of youth hostels. When we found a little dormitory we sat dormant, waiting for another train. I'd look out the unmoving windows while the girl slept or nursed or cried. I studied the shapes of natural and unnatural decorations on the land. I tried to imagine the shifting of huge plates under my feet and the rapid spinning through space. Later, endlessly, we'd climb back on a train—daytime, nighttime, or my early morning favorite—and watch the landscape spur and sputter, kaleidoscope through moving windows while the girl slept or nursed or cried. Movement always eased the pain. It was the hostels that tired me, the stopping, but it was the movement that kept me breathing, kept me real.

The revelation crept over me unlike a slap, unlike lightning, much like water across the basement floor. It was movement that was my home. It would never be the moment of exiting the train that would flush my cheeks and inspire me to the greatness I could feel pining inside me. It would always be the moment of embarking on a great journey, with no beginning and no end.

What This Mama Wants

Kristin Rowe-Finkbeiner

For my 31st birthday this mama would like a Lear jet, a castle, interesting conversation, ideas and books, a Lamborghini, linguine, dance classes every other night, the entire state of Alaska (just because it is the biggest), a personal chef, world peace and social justice, an art studio in downtown Seattle, moments to feel my own potential spark, permanently healthy and happy kids, a warm sunny island with a sandy beach, unlimited piña coladas, the perfect nanny, a secluded hideout to get a naked sunburn in all my lighter spots (with my husband to slowly rub yummy-smelling tanning oil in those very same spots), and late night disco dancing while my children sleep through the entire night without once waking. Nothing much.

But back to the reality of here and now on my home planet: Last year for my 30th birthday I took my newborn daughter, toddler son, mom-in-law, and husband to the tattoo parlor and got my belly pierced. I have been trying to think of another ACD for my all-too-soon 31st birthday (ACD = Anti-Conformity Device—a hidden token of pseudo-individuality in a capitalistic suburban consumer culture). Unfortunately, as much as I hate to admit it, the most attainable of my 31st birthday secret desires is a dreaded (dreaded because it seems to symbolize just the opposite of an ACD) kitchen mixer.

Oh, but it would be ever so useful. I secretly dream of mixing pizza dough faster and with less arm strain, although the true reason for the arm strain may have to do with a different kind of fatigue: the fatigue of never getting the 30 minutes needed to mix the dough alone with my own two arms, without one child or another drawing my attention. My husband suggested that maybe I could find a "hot-pink rhinestone-studded" mixer to satisfy my anti-establishment yearnings. But I have to face it: A kitchen mixer is a kitchen mixer is a kitchen mixer—and I do live in suburbia, with my two small children, a Republican husband, and a dog named Cowboy, all of whom I dearly love. All of them, that is, except the dog when his barking wakes my finally napping kids.

There is this terrible nagging fear that owning a kitchen mixer will lead me down that slippery slope of being so incredibly lost in diapers, grocery lists, sleep deprivation, and laundry that I won't even notice when I have fallen into sleepwalking through my own life. The phobia is that one small kitchen mixer will lead to a parade of overpriced kitchen appliances whose sole purpose is to wall me, the resident mama, into the kitchen.

I can just imagine an army of appliances marching down our cul-de-sac, heading straight to my little rambler. Bread machines dodging kids on tricycles. Cuisinarts getting in cutting contests with lawn mowers. All destined to wedge a poor mama into the last bit of space left in the kitchen, her voice muffled by the blender. The horror!

The truth is, mamahood is a miraculously mind-blowing, albeit sometimes mind-numbing, experience in good work. And it's no secret that being in the kitchen is also work (even if the commercials for dish detergent say otherwise while beckoning me to be their sudsy concubine). The challenge is to step over the pitfalls of stereotypical *Leave It to Beaver* households while taking the time to enjoy splashing with that cute cooing baby in the bathwater.

So back to the simple, secret birthday desires. When I think of it, the perfect 31st birthday present for this person who is also a mama might just be those 30 minutes alone, in daylight, with my own two arms, chocolate, riotous music, and a pen and paper. Hmmm . . . the possibilities. . . . But maybe I could also get that rhinestone-studded kitchen mixer after all.

Maybe kitchen mixers could be used for still bigger and better things. I could even start a movement with kitchen mixers. We could set up a foundation so that all mamas could have kitchen mixers. We could form a pizza co-op, only have to cook once a week, and feed our kids healthy pizza three times a day using those formerly dreaded appliances. Armed with kitchen mixers, we could end world hunger and champion much lesser causes like suburban alienation. I don't need an Anti-Conformity Device, I can *be* an Anti-Conformity Device.

Now, tell me—what do you really want for your next birthday?

Letters to the Editor

Weaning Does Suck

Dear Ariel,

Thank you so much for Keely Eastley's "Weaning Sucks" (Issue 12). This article could have been written by me, except that I'm still floundering around in indecision, caught in the push/pull between my son's needs and my own. It makes me sad that the act of nursing my son, which has been responsible for our very close relationship and has been so nurturing for both of us, has become a source of conflict for us. It is encouraging to hear that "cold turkey" can have such a positive outcome; my question for Keely is this: You say that after three days your son stopped asking for the breast, but at the end you say the process took three months. Can you clarify? I am still trying to determine how to wean my son humanely while saving my own sanity. I fear that if I wean abruptly, my son will feel betrayed, but if I let my son lead, I'll be doing this until he's in high school!

Mahalo for a great zine.

Aloha,

Gillian Culff

Kamuela, Hawaii

Editor's note: The whole process took three months—including the early limits she set and all of the back-and-forthing—but when she finally went cold turkey, he only asked to nurse for three days. Good luck!

With Every Kissed Boo-boo

Dear Hip Mamas,

I love, love, love this zine. I am comforted daily just knowing y'all are out there. I was inspired to write in the wake of recent violence (domestic and international) oozing from the U.S.A. It's really nuts out there, but every day we mamas get up and love our kids with all of our tolerant, groovy hearts. We are pushing back the evil with every kissed boo-boo, wiped nose, play dough pie, kindness to friend or stranger. We've got to keep making art and songs, mud pies and bubbles. Thank you!

Beth Mama

Sangerties, New York

The Beaver Taylor Bunch!

Dear Editors,

I recently heard about your publication through Glamour magazine. I am a mother of six beautiful, healthy children ages two, three, four, five, six, and eight years old. I am recently married after spending three and a half years as a single parent to my own children (the three-, six- and eight-year-olds). The other three are my stepchildren. After my divorce and coping alone with the death of my four-month-old daughter, I wish a publication like yours had been around for support sooner.

Laura Beaver Taylor

Lapeer, Michigan

Life in Mamaland

Girl,

Mamaland is all toothcut and rashpatrol. Will the real village please stand up? My roots have done laid tread marks long ago. My wardrobe is having an identity crisis. My self-expression desperately involves happy faces chewed into bologna slices, happy face "tattoos" drawn onto dishpan hands, and manic renditions of "If You're Happy and You Know It."

And yet, in spite of the cynical heebie-jeebies that creep up around all that happy talk, Mamaland is really really angel-breath on a mooncloud naptime, sunjoy, water rapture, belly laugh, insect delight, lightswitch magic, shadow dance, object personification, lullaby, and fullblast soul. I am a goddess and my baby is the pure reason.

Mamathings make sense, but they don't have to. Every tantrum has a silver lining and Huggies really are supreme. I never had so many wonderful moments to forget, lost in the speeding colors of my blooming babe.

Donnie-Marie

San Diego, California

Looking for Love

Sunday	Monday	Tuesday	Wednesday
3 Take kids to various fathers for visits. Go to farmers market for jam & squash.	**4** Clean house before CNN reporter comes over. Wear too much makeup.	**5** Cancel therapy. Fly with kid to NYC for indie media convention.	**6** Meet w/real mag publishers who have things like "schedules" & "budgets."
10 Try & write book, meet with publisher, get geeked out.	**11** Home: Take kids to protest. Try & explain riot cops.	**12** Cancel therapy. Take kids to amusement park. Up all night working.	**13** Watch anorexic babies falling on their poor heads doing Olympic gymnastics.
17 Shove laundry in closet before Mom visits. She still thinks place is a mess.	**18** Write raging commentary against president. Get more hate mail.	**19** Cancel therapy. Realize my life is a parody of a life.	**20** Hit back-to-school sale. Remember when stores had "salespeople."
24 Get new car, but it's anxiety-provoking: Doors randomly lock & unlock.	**25** Vow to give up coffee. Sleep til 3 P.M. Smoke cigarette, buy espresso.	**26** Cancel therapy. Cast spells on politicians. Buy "bruise"-colored nail polish.	**27** Buy Aveda hair shit. Trip on hair shit as internalized oppression.

Thursday	Friday	Saturday
	1 Quit smoking. Have random anxiety attacks all day.	**2** Smoke cigarette while wearing nicotine patch. Have anxiety attack about it.
7 Hang out on Lower East Side. Spend evening looking for Sesame Street.	**8** Still in NYC—try to find *James and the Giant Peach.*	**9** Take kid to see Statue of Liberty; go to friend's studio so she can record rap.
14 Still having random anxiety attacks & senseless shame spirals.	**15** Get nails done. Mope. Trip on manicures as internalized oppression.	**16** Go to Grandma's to eat yummy food & play in ocean. Get sunburned.
21 Try to figure out how we ended up with two lunch boxes & no backpack.	**22** Help kids build "Polly Pocket World." Muse about being 1/4-inch tall.	**23** Sweet-looking kids selling lemonade call me "lying bitch."
28 Decide everyone & their brother is a jerk.	**29** Read Jungian texts. Try & figure out my stage of initiation.	**30** Try to meditate. Mistake toy robot for my intuition. "Search & destroy!"

yo mama's daybook

Personals

Muriel Johnson

SBFWK

Me: single black female with kids, early 30s. Short, overweight, with lots of stretch marks. Looking for handsome male with great body, lots of money, able to accommodate all the desires and needs of a single woman and three children. Must enjoy nature, traveling, reading, dancing, and the arts, and be willing to pay all the time. Needs to be emotionally and financially secure, spiritually grounded, and a philanthropist-type. Must do laundry, dishes, general housecleaning, cooking, and assist with homework.

Must have a valid driver's license, an insured vehicle, preferably a minivan to taxi children to their various extracurricular activities. Must also be skilled in full-body massage and female pampering. Nonsmoker, no heavy drinking, no codependencies. Must expect nothing and give unconditionally. Can't wait to meet you!

The Dating Game

Spike Gillespie

Clichéd but true: Hairdressers know. Well, my hairdresser, anyway, knows. Nearly everything. For instance: About three trims ago, she was telling me the story of herself and her beau, a decent, funny guy who adores her. "The first date, I said to him, 'Look, I'm not interested in a guy who isn't going to stick around.'" My jaw dropped and my brows shot up so that she nearly cut an extra two inches off. Then, literally and figuratively, she set my head straight. She was tired of these elusive types. Sick of working for months, years even, only to be left with nothing, no one.

I'm listening and I'm thinking, *No way.* I get accused of moving too fast if, after a year of dating, I ask just once if he might consider sleeping over if I promise not to mention the possibility of going steady. I ask if she's worried that she might have scared him. "I didn't care," she said. And then, like the shampoo bottle says, she repeated. She wanted to sort through them as soon as possible and get to the, ahem, root of the relationship.

Three guys later, myself weary of the crap that some consider the delicate tango of compromise—she/me usually wanting more, he usually wanting less—I decided to try her frank approach. The next one would tell me, upfront, on date one, what he had in mind for the long haul. I met Andy, a columnist at the newspaper I occasionally contribute to. We did the email thing for a while and, though I was not profoundly attracted, I figured, *What the hell?* He was interested, he was cute, he was smart, and he was filthy rich. So, with an e-warning issued that he should not hit on me and a between-the-e-lines-message that maybe that was really a flirtatious challenge, I invited him over.

Welcome to the Wheel of Jeopardy, the real-life, updated version of the dating game. He came equipped with the following: two limes, two cigars (Cuban), and half a bottle of frozen Stoli (absolute truth in a bottle, if you will). Though we'd sworn this was just friendly, even an idiot could see what we were doing. It was a quest to determine, immediately, if we would win love's grand prize, or, instead, walk away with some lifelong supply of MSG-laden rice products with cable cars featured prominently on the box.

Contestant number one: me. How do you make money? Have any kids? Likes/dislikes? Freakish sexual fetishes? Favorite food? Desire to marry? Want any/more kids? And of course, You realize I'm just asking this out of polite, platonic curiosity, right? Contestant number two: him. Owns 22 hoagie shops; has two kids over 10; likes golf; dislikes discovering employees shooting up; has one never-used set of handcuffs in the dresser; likes spaghetti; maybe would marry; has a vasectomy; and yes, I know. His turn. My responses: fancy myself an artist; one kid; like smoking; hate assholes; more insatiable than freakish; like spaghetti; doubtful I'll marry; doubtful I'll have more kids.

We pause for a commercial break, another shot of vodka, and another squeeze of lime; cigar smoke is just sitting in a blue layer across the space above our heads. The judges in our heads are tallying things up. Ten points for kids. Fifteen for spaghetti. So, should we move on to the next round? I mean, now that we know all this and now that we're drunk, and in-the-sack compatibility is not an uncrucial factor. . . .

We don't. Well, okay, we did, but at a later date and only for a few weeks and it was good and proved there's more to life than kids and spaghetti but . . . crank up that consolation prize tune, will you? Hey, at least we're still friends. My split ends are out of control. I haven't had sex in months. Soon, I turn 32 and my family, the one that breathed a collective sigh of relief when I got pregnant, is going to revert to the theory that, since I've not married yet, I must be a lesbian after all. I need some advice.

I want a man. Really I do. Let me call the salon. There's gotta be a better way.

News Flash

The Statisticians Start to Wonder

A University of Chicago sex survey found that the average man has six partners in his lifetime and the average woman has two. If most men and women are heterosexual, as the study claims, then mathematically the average number of sex partners for men and women must be roughly the same. Where, then, do men get these four additional sex partners? Are they farm animals? Inflatable dolls? The researchers admit they "have no good answer" for the conundrum. (And we're all beginning to understand their findings—they're bogus.)

I Can't Figure Out How Passion Works: Melancholy in the Age of Recovery
Annie Downey

Who am I now? A fall skirt, a stream bent on becoming a river, time taking time, and never once myself. I hear things over and over again from all different mouths—my mother's, my friends', my partner's: You need to know what you want. You need to stop being so angry. You need to let go. You need to listen to your heart. None of this has done me much good.

I think when I hit 25 I figured that life wasn't going to someday wake up and get passionate. I wouldn't have this lover who would follow me around drooling over my sudden moves into flight, chasing me around corners into being. Have sex with me the way I jealously imagine everyone else is having. I eye cucumbers nervously. Will I become this cliché, I wonder . . . will I become one of those women you find on calendars in joke stores . . . and will it be "just fine." I think about getting a lover. I think about placing one of those personal ads that I used to read for a bit of fun with friends: *SWF, 25, needs a little pick-me-up after the kids go to bed. Must be discreet and share similar interests: coffee and cigarettes. Hate mustaches.*

My friend answered a personal ad and the guy was downright frightening. Now she surfs the Internet playing S&M games with other married miserable people who haven't had sex in a couple of years either. She says it's great, that even when she's in her nightgown and hasn't showered in three days, she feels attractive. She says, "I got it going on." She says it's just an easy way to meet guys after her children get tucked in. I say, "But what about so-and-so?" She says he doesn't even care, that he thinks it's a big joke and people don't really tie each other up: "Who would be that sick?" She says that lack of sex makes you psychotic. I say, "Yeah, I guess so."

I got a pedicure before my baby was due. I thought that even if I looked like shit, the doctors would think I had great toes. This was tied in with my dignity. But anyhow, my appointment was with this woman whose fiancé had just had a heart attack, but she really didn't feel anything—because she wasn't that in love with him and because she was still in love with her ex. I kept saying, "Are you sure this is all right? Are you sure? If you need to cancel . . ." "No, No," she said. "I'm just fine."

So we start talking and I'm lying about my life—I do this when I go into salons. It's mainly to keep her interested because I feel guilty that she's painting my toenails, like I couldn't do it. Anyway, we start talking about sex and *the lack thereof,* and I say, "Did you ever notice when you're not *getting any,* that you shop a lot? You're, like, manic about it." And she says, "Yeah, you start to spend compulsively; you become a *compulsive spender.*"

Everyone likes to say "compulsive"—also "neurotic," "chronic," "pseudo," and "codependent." Our mottoes are all tied to "the self": self-help groups, finding the inner self, self-recovery, the self within, self-help lines. What is a "self"? Do we all of a sudden find our "self" in a Dumpster behind a 7-Eleven?

Did you ever notice how nobody in a past life was anything boring? They're always servants, harem girls, Indians, or slaves. They're good, kind. They're victims, and that is why in this life they have so much pain. One of my very rich, very white Southern friends was told by a "trusted" psychic that she had been this poor single black mother who had died young and left many children behind, who were still living. This "trusted" psychic gave her the name and town where this woman had lived. My friend in turn looked her "living" children up, and she said it was odd, that she had felt the connection right away to the name and place but was stunned to find herself not welcome in her children's houses. She visited her grave anyway; it was unkempt; she had cried and cried. She said, "It is my lesson in this life to not forget the neglect and pain of those forgotten."

Why is it that we must have a past other than our own? I think we are bored, bored with what we got, bored with what we have. I, too, once believed I was an Indian who had done something terrible to my tribe, and this was my karma. I learned about this from my aunt who was doing Rohan work on me. She took imaginary daggers out of my uterus, chains from my neck, and bullets from my back (where the "white men" had shot me). She performed hours of therapy—gasping, chanting, pulling, grunting.

I have stood for hours in the shower imagining white light pouring down on me, cleansing my soul. I've interpreted my dreams. I have talked with my inner child in the middle of my kitchen. I've tried creative therapies of all types. I have rebirthed. Learned to channel my sexual energy to my heart source. Done aromatherapy for beginners. Run with Artemis. Walked in the woods naked. Danced with peaches in a wedding dress. Had psychotherapy for five years. Almost gotten a prescription for Prozac. Gone through marriage counseling even though I'm not married. Joined Al-Anon . . . AA . . . OA . . . SA . . . ACOA . . . confronted my father, but not my mother.

My friend who surfs the Internet found a lover. She told me in whispers about how she met him in the park with no underwear. How he catered to her all night long. I asked her if they had safe sex. She said, "Yes, of course." I asked her if the sex was good. She said, "The best." I felt as if I were drowning. I wonder if I can survive a long-term relationship in which everything risky becomes comfortable.

I used to panic and run to my analyst, dreaming up things to be passionate about. We used to dissect my relationships into power struggles until they became dead, unmoving. I would find frustration and relax. I was sure my partner didn't love me. I was sure he was having an affair. I used to run from my noon AA meeting, pushing the baby stroller through mounds of snow to his office.

I watch *Oprah* now instead of running. I curl up on the couch with my son and watch people from all over share their misery on national television. I learn about EQ, how friends hate each other over a few pounds, how some women wear makeup to bed, the warning signs that "he" is having an affair, and "fabulous" makeovers you can do at home for your "self." I can't figure out what button to push. I can't figure out how passion works. I keep thinking one day I'll wake up and it will come again. I'll begin to paint and write. I'll feel "in love." Do days just go by, into one another? Closing down. I opened a door today and thought,

When I'm old, even this simple opening will be difficult. I should be grateful. But I'm not.

Who am I now? A woman with two small children, beautiful babies, my babies. I want to get high. I want to listen to old Irish ballads. I want to watch *An Angel at My Table.* I want—something—to get over my "self."

Who am I? A bent half with no beginning . . . borrowed time . . . soft rhyme . . . pregnant belly . . . jam not jelly . . . aching tooth . . . scratchy record . . . rent not paid on the first?

Terrible, isn't it? Not really.

Twenty-five years looking and never finding. I know people have spent longer in wheelchairs, in doorways, in cars, in boxes, in sanity, in marriage. Hey, but isn't this the age of recovery? Of *self?* And resurrection, horoscopes, channeling, chakras, readings, sightings, findings? What do I have to recover—my daddy's fingers on my body, lips exposed? My mama not believing; my lover not interested?

Aren't I interesting, darling? Don't I play the victim well? Don't you want to save me?

Tell me that I don't look fat. Tell me what clothes I should wear. Tell me my stretch marks don't really show. Tell me, tell me, tell me . . . I'm still beautiful.

Single Moms OK

June Day

have to admit it. I read the personals. Even while I was knocking boots with Ideal last year and discussing the inevitable wedding, I was reading the personals. It's one to two parts curiosity, and another part either reminder or possibility, depending on my mood and circumstance. A reminder of who I could dial late on a Sunday, or on a Tuesday afternoon. The seduction is in the artificiality of the arrangement; to pair oneself with that mysterious stanza of black print. To pair oneself with a stranger.

Now that I'm single, the joy of reading the personals has diminished to a shame. I read them less, and more critically. If everyone really likes long walks, quiet dinners, candlelight, dancing, Sundays with the paper, and snuggling, why are things so complicated? Reading the personals leaves me with the bitter sense that everyone is either exactly the same (garnished with different heights, colors, and marital histories) or posing for the camera. What are they so afraid of? Why won't they show themselves, even with the protective layer of an anonymous box number?

I read them tonight, my daughter asleep in the next room. I decided to count how many were seeking me, by vague definition: attractive, female, 20s, but fun times? I can't be sure what that entails. Another ad reads, "seeking anybody"; it's a hit, but too desperate, not in the tally. By the second column I'm getting nervous: *Shit, I'm hotter than Georgia asphalt and I only have one check.* I shut my eyes and silently list my credentials: good hair, easy on the eyes, hyperacademic achiever, independent, perfect mother with better child, I like every food but coconut, all kinds of loving and generous to boot, I even make the grocery store fun. . . . But the trend isn't elusive; it's easy to trace. Most matches say "no kids," or imply no mamas, no substance, nothing serious. A few ads take on a generous spirit and proclaim, "Single Moms OK." *Hot damn!* Thanks heaps. The "problem" is my daughter—my daughter the genius, my daughter the talented, my daughter the asset. "Single Moms OK." An equal dating opportunity. Oh sure, kids equal responsibility and who needs it? But my daughter? A burden? She's better than any fool writing a personal ad. So good night, independent menfolk of the planet. And may your search for barren women be fruitful.

Murder of a Jumping Bean: A True Tale of Pregnancy Hormones

Girl-Mom Ann-Marie Keene

I don't wanna go home," I said to my love, Charlie, as I packed my things to go back to Maine after a great visit with him in Boston. "Every time I get used to being here, I have to go home."

"I know," he sighed. "It'll be better when I move back and we're together again, right? Just think about that when you get lonely."

He gave me a kiss goodbye and some money, then left for work.

It was a muggy day in the city—something that makes being pregnant very annoying. I hopped into the shower—a long, cold shower—and got ready to go see him at work. I always make sure to see him on his break, but I purposely get there early to make sure no chicks are hitting on him. I like some of the people he works with, so I pretend to have conversations with them, but I'm actually spying on him and he knows it.

The train is crowded. I feel like I'm about to pass out. Can't these folks see I'm pregnant? I try to poke my belly out more in the hopes that someone might give me a seat. After about five stops, with more and more people getting on, I finally get off. Free at last!

I run up the stairs, then walk down Commonwealth Avenue to Planet Records. On the way, I see my favorite street folk, Butch. He's so funny. We talk a bit and I give him a dollar, even though I know he'll spend it on booze.

On Charlie's break, we go to eat at the Deli Haus, my favorite spot for mashed potatoes and gravy. The gravy is just *so* good! I think about things while I'm eating my potatoes. At this moment, there is no wrong; there is only gravy. I would do anything now, as long as I could keep eating. *I'd marry him*, I think to myself. *He's so good to me, getting me mashed potatoes with my favorite gravy in the world. I have to keep this guy.*

The look on his face as I inhale my food is just darling. I can tell he's thinking the same thing I am. Something like, *Wow. If she's this happy about gravy, it won't take much to make her happy for the rest of her life.*

We get back to the record store, late again, but the manager is pretty cool, so he gets over it. To make sure Charlie doesn't get into any unwanted trouble, I decide to leave instead of spying. I go to a smoke shop down the street where they sell $5,000 bongs. I think if anyone spent that much money on a bong, they'd have nothing to smoke in it.

I see a big box of Mexican jumping beans with a sign that says 4 Free. More Than 4 and You're Out The Door! I quickly grab four of the liveliest ones I can find and leave.

I head back to Planet Records to show off my new treasure. A weirdo customer gets into a conversation with me about what makes them jump. We agree that it's some sort of insect or worm living inside, but no one else in the store believes us, so I get Charlie to cut one open on the counter. There it is, a little wormy larvae of some sort. We all decide we should free it, so I pick it up, still in the bean, and I start to say goodbye again.

That's when I drop it on the floor.

Pretty soon the whole store is looking for it.

I feel something squish under my foot. I look down to see the remains between my sandal and my toe. I think I might puke and I feel really ashamed, so I keep quiet about it. I go on helping everyone look for it and keep saying things like "I don't understand—it couldn't have been that fast!"

I don't know why I can't say that I killed it. It was just a stupid jumping bean I got from the smoke shop. Nothing major. But I feel like I've committed murder. It was an accidental killing, I try to tell myself, but I keep crawling around on my hands and knees pretending to look for the damn thing until we all decide to give up.

I kiss Charlie and go off to catch my bus back home.

A few days later, I call Charlie and say I have something important to talk to him about. I'm almost crying. I blurt out everything. How the larvae thing got stuck between my toe and my sandal, how I killed it and didn't say anything.

He laughs so hard I think he might pee his pants.

I feel more and more horrible. "You jerk!" I scream into the phone. "I need some mashed potatoes and gravy from the Deli Haus right now!"

He goes all quiet, like a little boy, and says, "I love you."

News Flash

There Oughta Be a Law . . .
American Sex Laws Currently on the Books

In the quiet town of Connorsville, Wisconsin, it's illegal for a man to shoot off a gun when his female partner has an orgasm.

It's against the law in Willowdale, Oregon, for a husband to curse during sex.

In Oblong, Illinois, it's punishable by law to make love while hunting or fishing on your wedding day.

No man is allowed to make love to his wife with the smell of garlic, onions, or sardines on his breath in Alexandria, Minnesota. The law says he must brush his teeth upon request.

Warn your hubby that after lovemaking in Ames, Iowa, he isn't allowed to take more than three gulps of beer while lying in bed with you or holding you in his arms. As with many of these laws, if you're not married, you're not protected.

Bozeman, Montana, has a law that bans all sexual activity in the front yard of a home after sundown between members of the opposite sex if they're nude. (Wear socks!)

In hotels in Sioux Falls, South Dakota, every room is required to have twin beds. And the beds must always be a minimum of two feet apart when a couple rents a room for only one night. And it's illegal to make love on the floor between the beds!

The owner of every hotel in Hastings, Nebraska, is required to provide each guest with a clean and pressed nightshirt. No couple, even if they are married, may sleep together in the nude. Nor may they have sex unless they are wearing one of these clean white cotton nightshirts.

An ordinance in Newcastle, Wyoming, specifically bans couples from having sex while standing inside a store's walk-in meat freezer.

In Norfolk, Virginia, a woman can't go out without wearing a corset. (There was once a civil-service job—for men only—called a corset inspector.)

However, in Merryville, Missouri, women are prohibited from wearing corsets because "the privilege of admiring the curvaceous, unencumbered body of a young woman should not be denied to the normal, red-blooded American male." (And yes, this and the previous law are *really* currently on the books.)

A Florida law: If you're a single, divorced, or widowed woman, you can't parachute on Sunday afternoons.

No woman may have sex with a man while riding in an ambulance within the boundaries of Trementon, Utah. If caught, the woman can be charged with a sexual misdemeanor and "her name is to be published in the local newspaper." The man isn't charged, nor is his name revealed.

Letting Go

Yantra Bertelli

Tuesday, December 5

From their mouths to my lips and every yellow-green blade of grass choking in the front lawn, a pause and the same-old empty gnaw. The sky is clear, cold, and waiting for morning. I wouldn't mind chalking up this day to whiny garble and getting on to better things. The repetition swirls and I pull close. There is laundry, always sheets because the son cries, the mother wakes, rocks, bottles, lies back down, and tries for sleep once more. Again and again knowing that someday the click of the light will be her last movement in their room for the rest of the night. But she is here, I am here, and the nights lead to soakings. Their mouths whisper and my lips sing and the grass dies because it's too cold for everything and we miss the sun.

From their chins to my hips and every brittle branch cutting itself from the tree full of fungus, a silenced and jagged glance to the sky. The falling limbs breaking air make no sound and I wonder if my own silence crackles with the same brilliance. My legs pull me to the corner, waving, my calves ache and I've forgotten to pay attention. I realize that I'm running out of time and force inspiration, finding asphalt more attractive and my ears frozen under a beanie cap. I run for sanity and they nod, kissable chins and sparkling eyes; it's a pity that Mama can't seem to roll around in their beauty enough to coat her nag. My hips carry me away and I mumble my irritations, enjoy their smooth, and ignore everything in between.

From their feet to my fingertips, I wake this morning sore from pounding, worry, and playing hooky from sleep. The phone rings. I hate the phone waking me up; it rings into my dreams and her footsteps run to discover who is at the other end. Nana or work, never sweet voices behind that thing. Work. She plants her cold feet on my thigh as the question-answering commences and she crawls under the covers to giggle. I'm tired of being interrupted in sleep, thought, and movement as peace of mind garbles into nothing. It's time to start again—my fingertips run themselves against cheekbones and I pull wool socks up to my knees—time to welcome the neighbor's barking dog.

Monday, December 11
You ask what is wrong. You ask if the kids' other mom "said" something, if she is taking my patience for yet another joyride. You get a gleam in your eye when she fucks up. I don't want to be part of your sentiment, Mother, and refuse to feel comfort in your judgment. My life has been scrutinized with that same odd inquiry. You want to comfort me, to hug me, to give me advice; I want to heave all over your lap and weep. It's not your words. It's your tone. Everything that you say is measured and precise, even kind. The life you give each sound inspires a sharpness that rips across my chest. I should thank you. I should appreciate your help, your love for my children. I should, but the strings are cutting off my air.

"Stop fucking with me!"

Thursday, December 14

My bubble: translucent, layered, hard. I smack my head against the boundaries again and again. The welts rarely surface, bruising just below skin, lingering in nerves. I created this tidy existence, gagged the world, and covered my ears. Now there are six ears instead of two, six ears and two hands. I reach to shield them from voices, ill prepared, hate flooding into my naked thoughts.

Our little family made the paper today. A big picture and lots of tiny words with a few larger ones sprinkled in: "queer" and "lesbian." Not our first brush with the media or a public acknowledgment of our "alternative" family. It's not big news. It's been done. I'm not used to hiding or screwing around with shame concerning my identity. *Dyke* isn't painted on my clothes or shaved in my scalp, but I am out, out, out, out and have been for more than 10 years.

I got a call from my mother and let the machine answer the phone. The machine is our official greeter, considering that 80 percent of the calls received are from her or the ex. "Hi honey, just wanted to let you know that you are in the paper today. [A silent pause.] We saw it and Dad and I thought the picture was NICE." Translation: "Hi honey, we saw that article in the paper—you know, the one that you told us about? We can't believe that you are waving this whole QUEER issue in the air for all of our friends and family to see again." I thought about the call for a moment and went on with the day.

She called again later and we talked. She says volumes with her tone instead of actual words, a typical Mom maneuver. She mentions the article again, noting that her friends at church commented that it was good to get to see the kids. Being that I am a big old sinner and all, I guess it wasn't good to see me.

This isn't new. I should expect it; why today of all days does it dig? Perhaps because the article wasn't even about being a queer mama? Perhaps their fear irritates my rather sensitive neck with all that choking? Or could it be because I am strong, creative, driven, and a loving mother whom they will merely "tolerate" due to my glaring wrongs? My parents can't see me. They can't see me and it's infuriating that it still pulls tears from my eyes and drives betrayal into my faraway memories.

I have never had to care about the world. I've had my own pairs of disapproving eyes peering inside my life day in and day out. The world can't hurt me like they have hurt me. It's easy to toss my life and struggles onto paper because I have nothing to lose. It's easy to pull my lover's middle close and kiss her in public, when rejection is this familiar. The face of fear is all too familiar.

I don't know if I'm brave, proud, or bitter: a bit of all three, I suspect. Early in life I was alone; necessity taught to me to find my center and grow the ability to filter out negativity. I saved myself. Now I have these little souls that I am responsible for. Inside miniature bodies, huge spirits that love wide and lack the heavy calluses needed to avoid being silenced. I am forced to pay attention to the hate I ignored before, listening because they are listening.

My bubble: translucent, layered, hard. It does not protect them. It confines me, trapping us both in an illusion of freedom. My hands fall to my sides. No motion can remove hate from the air. My palms cradle their fingers. We link hands, close our eyes, and exist.

Tuesday, December 19

His shoe loses leather at its toe, exposing white threads. A worn size seven hand-me-down wardrobe must do for child number two. Her bedtime ritual lacks closeness at a crucial turn, peeling away lasting comfort, an anxious hand-me-down and the same old song faced nightly for child number one. My thirst for repetition churns gold at its peak, irritating saliva, sticky and burning a hole, night's familiar hand-me-down searing clean for this mother squinting in darkness.

I tell myself that it doesn't matter and I know what I am looking for as I turn around and ask a thousand questions. I don't know who to trust or if the exercise has any value or meaning to the raw flesh underneath my feet. When I see my eyes and the tapered hair at the bottom of my neck, I wonder how moments can shift immediately to the left or fall against huge curves ticking away wrinkles forming in my brow.

Here I am facing stripes and the sag of time collecting near my ears. Shoulders fall, smacking my big toe and creating a huge hematoma, but it's all in my head and the blood doesn't exist. Just the bump. Just the noticeable lump under the leopard-print socks the neighbor gave me for my birthday. I curl my toes and try to shove my foot inside my boots, walking on heels, bringing caution to pain. I spin and I forget the pretend ache and the lack of blood, landing face-down on the couch.

I reach for the up and down, then stop. Sitting up, I find my shoulders and the music, begging the note to hold and the song to start over again so I can connect to the constant hum inside my skin. My toe throbs. The song starts, and a veil cascades over my eyes as I bury my face in the couch. The smell of the cushion, my children, years meeting notes; I forget everything past my cunt and cry when the display reads zero.

I push the button again because I want it to be that easy. I want it to be that easy and the color to be clear and not a color, the throb to pound inside my heart, not my toe, and to see the lump so my mind doesn't have to wonder if I'm pretending. My eyes hit their reflection and my ridiculousness follows the lines covering my stomach as I cross my arms to touch my hips. The repetition hardens my nipples, but the gold is in my head and I have no sound.

Sunday, December 24

"I'm praying you will embrace the peace that only God can give."

Grandma is spreading holiday cheer again! Her dear queer grand-daughter is knee-deep in sin and she wants to reassure me that who I am doesn't "change her love" for me. Grandma fails to realize that her message tucked away inside well-meaning breeds hate. Grandma doesn't see that she feeds into the fear lunging from throats to ears, to my children who know the truth and are confused by her lies. Grandma wants to save me. She doesn't want to see me.

If I struggle in my life, it's because I'm queer. If I cry by myself in my bedroom, it's because I'm queer. If my relationships fall apart, it's because I'm queer. If I gain weight, it's because I'm queer. If I lose weight, it's because I'm queer. If I call myself strong, it's because I'm queer and defensive. If I ask for space, it's because I'm queer, defensive, and ashamed. If I withdraw from hate, anger, and betrayal, it's because I'm queer, defensive, ashamed, and searching for acceptance.

No wonder I'm a perfectionist. No wonder I'm afraid of fucking up.

Under her plan I don't get to think for myself, love myself, or open myself to another soul. I'm not allowed to make choices and my passions are always misguided. My words are slanderous. My life means nothing. All the energy I give to living means nothing. I am nothing. I hear you. I am not acceptable.

Who you are, Grandma, doesn't change my love for you. What you do changes my capacity to look upon your eyes. I am true to myself and my children. I am true to passion and a journey thick with tension and struggle. I can't believe I still have tears, but I do. They fall as a reminder that I have to let go. You choose not to see who I am and I refuse to extend my hand to you and ask for nothing.

Tuesday, December 26

When I was four years old, I learned to ride a bike. I can't recall the struggle of that experience, the attempts, or the scrapes. What I do remember was my blue bike with tall handlebars, a sparkling banana seat, and the once-in-a-while opportunity to ride free in my grandmother's court. My parents' freedom was found in communal living and whole wheat bread. Their rebellion concerned appearance, where they lived, and what they chose to put into their mouths. Even at four I wanted more.

I wanted the open road, or at least newly paved suburban asphalt, with little traffic and hair that wasn't fastened tightly into braids, ponytails, or a bun. I didn't want to be in my mother's line of vision at all times, due to her fear of the less-stable element in our community. I wanted for her spirit, her freedom, for something lighter than cooking everything from scratch, washing clothes in the sink, and her constant arguments with red clay dirt and my clothes.

I wonder what my kids want for me? Less irritation behind my daily requests? More time in my arms or sprawled out on the floor so they each can pick a section of my body to melt against? A bit more fun and a little less mom? A mom who can crawl from behind her own thoughts and pull laughter from air?

My daughter is four and she can ride a bike. I can recall her entire struggle and determination to whirl around her grandmother's block.

Her bike is blue, minus the high handlebars and banana seat. She enjoys the audience of my parents, the clapping, the unreasonable amount of attention they lavish on her every word. She occasionally informs me of her grandparents' beliefs, and to my amazement I'm kind and to the point with my responses. I can see her spinning with it all. Why don't they see eye to eye? Why are they so private? Why isn't there one answer? I push stereotypes, boundaries, internal skepticism, and truth, wrestling with myself against the annoyance of socialization. I wonder what she wants for me. I wonder what *more* is at her four.

I want the open road for my children. I want freedom that isn't wound around their sexual identities, their bodies, or where they live. I want their challenges to be of their choosing, their longings heavy with passion, not reactions to my lack of vision. I want their inspiration, yet in the back of my head and nestled into the corners of my heart, I know that I am their mother, and part of their journey is always going to be about letting go of me.

News Flash

Gyration Inspector Needed

There was no smoking. There was no drinking. There were plenty of chaperones. But in 1996, for the first time in 151 years, there was dancing at Baylor University in Waco, Texas.

In late January, the school's new president, Robert B. Sloan Jr., casually told students during a question-and-answer session that he had decided to permit dancing at the university, whose Baptist roots are among the deepest in the country.

"The real question for us is the kind of dancing," Sloan, 43, said.

But not everyone was pleased with the dancing move. "Who's going to be the gyration inspector?" asked Miles Seaborn, president of the Southern Baptist Church in Fort Worth. "Are they going to have a committee, or is the president going to do it? Baylor has been on the slippery slope for some time, and this is just one more slip. Wherever modern dancing is, there is alcohol and promiscuousness."

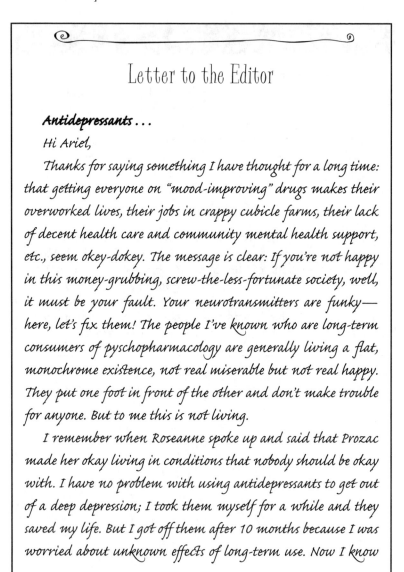

Letter to the Editor

Antidepressants...

Hi Ariel,

Thanks for saying something I have thought for a long time: that getting everyone on "mood-improving" drugs makes their overworked lives, their jobs in crappy cubicle farms, their lack of decent health care and community mental health support, etc., seem okey-dokey. The message is clear: If you're not happy in this money-grubbing, screw-the-less-fortunate society, well, it must be your fault. Your neurotransmitters are funky— here, let's fix them! The people I've known who are long-term consumers of pyschopharmacology are generally living a flat, monochrome existence, not real miserable but not real happy. They put one foot in front of the other and don't make trouble for anyone. But to me this is not living.

I remember when Roseanne spoke up and said that Prozac made her okay living in conditions that nobody should be okay with. I have no problem with using antidepressants to get out of a deep depression; I took them myself for a while and they saved my life. But I got off them after 10 months because I was worried about unknown effects of long-term use. Now I know people who have been on Prozac for 10 years. And the experience did have after effects for me: a continuing "brownout" mood where I was never deeply depressed but never happy either, and a full seven years of my sex drive taking a hike.

Now I'm having a lot of trouble with menopausal depressiveness and having terrible anxiety attacks. I have dealt with depression for a long time via Zen rather than pills, and I am trying to deal with the anxiety as well, but I find everyone tells me to "get on Prozac" or "take Xanax." When I say I don't want to, they say I'm "refusing help." The help I want is support for my drugless way of dealing with my emotions, not a handful of prescriptions, but I'm finding that hard to come by. If you don't want to take pills then you must "want" to feel bad. Hello!

Anyway, thanks for saying it. With antidepressants and anxiolytics to control the adults and Ritalin to dampen any independent spirit on the part of the kids (and eliminate the need for educational reform—it's not the system, it's the kid), America Inc.™ should have no fears of any significant objection to its program of advancing corporate interest and eroding individual rights.

Chris
California

The Parental Is Political

TNT Jackson

SHE'LL PUT YOU IN TRACTION.

ACME PORTABLE MILKER

VANESSA.

① DISCO MATERNITY DRESS
② ENGORGEMENT CAN QUICKLY RUIN A GIRL'S EVENING OR FOIL
A PLOT; ALWAYS CARRY THE BREAST PUMP.
③ ...CUZ NO MAMA EVER TOOK OVER THE STATE CAPITOL WITH A BUTTERKNIFE
④ PRE-NATAL VITAMINS
⑤ SKI-MASK FOR IMPROMPTU BANK ROBBERIES AND OTHER GUERRILLA ACTIVITIES WHERE
HOSTAGES MAY BE INVOLVED.

Sunday	Monday	Tuesday	Wednesday
1 Take kids to various fathers for visits. Find out one dad's left town. Feel duped.	**2** Try & convince mortgage broker I make 2K a month. (Lie like a dog.)	**3** Cancel therapy. Apply for seven jobs, including "thesis ghostwriter" & "cereal taster."	**4** Get temp job where co-workers call Newt Gingrich "our boy."
8 Drive hours down Hwy 1 to go to Santa Cruz Boardwalk. Closed!	**9** Get $1,036 parking ticket. Attempt to flee country.	**10** Cancel therapy. Get asked by hipster "how old" my tattoos are.	**11** Kids take over "Hip Mama Hour" on Free Radio Berkeley.
15 Spend day wondering what's unpredictable about moon & tides.	**16** Drive to Las Vegas. Win $500. Kids spend $250 in arcade.	**17** Feel like I'm on psychotropic drugs. Realize it's just Circus Circus.	**18** Go see white tigers. Pass out in 120-degree weather.
22 Tell first grader she doesn't have to pledge allegiance to flag (eye roll).	**23** Propose to Edwidge Danticat via email. No response.	**24** Cancel therapy. Get flu shot in Kmart parking lot.	**25** Break bad on ex at his workplace. Narrowly escape arrest.
29 Take kids to various fathers for visits. Get fired from phone sex job.	**30** First grader wins school prize for patriotism. Decide to move to Canada.	**31** Cancel therapy. Make plans to have another baby.	

Thursday	Friday	Saturday
5 Resist urge to dump unasked-for advice on pregnant co-worker.	**6** Give in to urge. Tell her to dump man. She stops speaking to me.	**7** Secured credit card maxed out. Write bad check for new coat for kid.
12 Astrologist sez: "Your inner nature is irreconcilable with your outer nature."	**13** Host double birthday party with 30 five-year-olds & Clover the Clown.	**14** Astro chart sez: "You're unpredictable like the moon & tides."
19 Win $250 in quarters. Spend it on room service. (one pizza, two salads.)	**20** Get stuck in Bakersfield. Pay for motel room in quarters.	**21** Head home w/ just enough quarters for laundry.
26 Find out "friendly neighbor" is actually born-again Christian.	**27** Second grader gets busted for bringing "knife" to school. It's a nail file.	**28** Scrub walls. Dye hair red. Buy new Witches' Almanac.

yo mama's daybook

Yo Mama for President

End Patriarchy as We Know It! Vote Yo Mama!

Tired of voting for a lesser of two evils? Sick of the same old Texas billionaire alternative? Tired of white guys in ugly suits running the whole show? Sick and tired of the whole pathetic deal? We are, too. But don't stay home this election year—write in Yo Mama. She promises to revolutionize government from top to bottom:

A meaningful job and minimum income for everyone. Or stay home if you want; Yo Mama will guarantee you livable child support for raising happy, healthy kids.

Minimum wage? Who cares? What we really need is maximum wage to solve the lazy rich people/high cost of living problem.

Marriage for anyone—straight, gay, or lesbian—who chooses to go down that scary path.

Gays in the military? Sorry. Yo Mama will abolish the military. Why blow up people we don't even know in other countries? The Pentagon's budget will be reallocated toward universal health care, universal child care, quality public education, and to guarantee the absolute right to food, shelter, clean air and water, and good pizza and ice cream—delivered.

What for the ultraconservatives, you ask? Yo Mama will offer free passage into the burning depths of hell for all right-wing dittoheads. She'll even throw a prayer breakfast going-away party.

Worried about the future of safe, legal abortion? Fear not: Yo Mama promises free abortion on demand. She knows what's up. She has no business in your uterus. Women are not incubators. Fetuses are not babies. Abortion is not murder.

And Yo Mama's response to domestic violence? This president will never ask, "Why doesn't she leave?" She'll make him leave. There will only be two options for batterers: graduate from an approved overcoming-violence program or be exiled into hell with the dittoheads, where both will be haunted by volunteer welfare queens and the ghosts of dead social-policy victims.

Had it with ridiculous family court decisions? Family issues and decisions on child custody will be taken out of the courts and given to a council of our feminist grandmothers. Come to think of it, she'll replace all courts with a wise grandma posse. Anyone who doesn't like it can go . . . you guessed it . . . to hell!

And this is just the beginning, girlfriends.

Yo Mama sounds like a crazy commie, you say? Perhaps she is and perhaps she isn't. She's a mama, and she won't stand by and watch her children starve while the politicians in Washington sound like the invisible grownups in *Peanuts* cartoons: "Wha-wha-wha, wha-wha-wha, ha-wha-wha."

Wondering how she'll accomplish all this? Then you're being too damn practical, girlfriends. And, anyway, rumor has it Yo Mama has something no other politician can lay claim to: a functioning brain and a magic wand.

Read her hips: She's from a place called Reality. She'll end patriarchy as we know it, offer tax breaks for all the radical fringe activists, and guarantee a tasty tofu stir-fry in every pot.

Ne̊ẘs Flash

Right to Bear a Nose Stud

When Heather Gray turned 13, she and her mother agreed a nosepiercing would be an appropriate rite of passage, but when Heather showed up at John Muir Middle School in Burbank, California, officials ordered the removal of the discreet stud. The school nurse, citing hygiene concerns, removed the offending nose stud on a Monday in September.

On Tuesday, Heather was back at school, the stud was back in her nose, and she had an extra supply of studs in her pocket just in case school officials confiscated the one in her nose.

"I don't think they should tell me how many holes I can have in my face," Heather told the local newspaper later that week. And they don't anymore, thanks to Heather and her mother's persistence.

"They messed with the wrong person," said Nancy Gray, Heather's mother and owner of Burbank's Java Goddess store and café. "I'm trying to give her a lesson in activism and First Amendment rights. Basically, her nose ring pissed off some conservative and they made her take it out."

The lesson included a "no retreat" policy on the nose stud, a trip to the ACLU, an interview with one of the school counselors, and a family laugh at a letter that appeared in the local paper scolding Nancy, "It would be far better for Mrs. [sic] Gray to teach her daughter respect for authority rather than rebellious activism."

How to Raise a Draft Dodger

Leslie Gore Interviews Utah Phillips

Folk icon Utah Phillips sings songs about union organizing, loafing in America, and, yes, raising his kids. He talked to *Hip Mama's* Leslie Gore from his home in Nevada City, California, in the spring of 1999.

Leslie: How can we teach our children how to opt out of all the violence that will be available to them in life?

Utah: Well, it's a given. Look out at the world as it is. The obvious leaps forth at you—although we're not inclined to admit it. The single greatest similarity between the Rwandan massacre, what was going on in Bosnia and now in Kosovo, in El Salvador and in Guatemala, the thing they all have in common is that it's young men being violent. And unless men own up to that, it's just going to continue. The basic question is: Why do men kill? Unless we get to that . . . Littleton, Colorado, it's the same thing. We don't have a problem of international warfare; we have a male problem. Unless we can deal with it on basic terms we're not going to deal with it at all. Why do men kill? I can't believe that it's genetic, I just can't live with that; there's no hope in that theory, and I refuse to live without hope. I don't know. There hasn't been a lot of work done on this subject. There is a lot about how to raise a nonviolent child, about passive action, nonviolent direct action, the Catholic Worker girl—she was the most powerful woman this country ever turned out—but there is a *great silence* about why men kill. Why is it that we don't want to talk about it? I mean, look at this whole thing with Littleton: The general response to all this is *more punishment*. Let's make the schools more like prisons, let's make more prisons . . . well, that's just more violence, the violence just perpetuates itself. It's hard to find out where it begins and where it ends. My guess is that it starts with kids. We should be teaching nonviolent problem-solving in school. Within the system we could have parents and children coming together and finding out how to be nonviolent.

Michael True of the Assumption College in Worcester, Massachusetts, has written about how to raise a nonviolent child, but, you see, he is already a practicing pacifist. Nonviolence isn't a list of rules that you can follow; it's a way of life. The real work is in choosing that path. My feeling is that the groundwork is laid when we're real little kids. That's when we start becoming aware of anger, rage, and violent action. What can we expect? This is especially true with males, don't you think? Do you know why? Now you just keep asking that question, my friend, because when we figure that out, the bodies will stop falling. If we don't, it's just going to keep happening, over and over.

Leslie: What do you think of television?

Utah: Now, you can quote me on this: The two most dangerous books in the world are the Bible and the *TV Guide*. Now, the Bible is just a big long book of excuses that gives you license to do some damn ugly things. And then you just say, "Well, it's in the Bible. . . ." It is a catalog of human abuses. And the *TV Guide* is all about the ugly, rapacious way that capitalism plugs our heads. Now what you do is you take your television and you throw it out into the middle of the street. That should be your last violent act. And then you can sit down with your kids and start singing songs, and you tell them stories, and you can make kites together, you can go on long walks, and you can build toys.

Leslie: We want our children to be in the middle of things, to come face to face with things in life, so that they may have the radicalizing experiences necessary to form convictions and beliefs, but we don't want them to get hurt. We want to protect them from harm.

Utah: Now, you can't have an omelet without breaking eggs. The same is true in confronting evil. Martin Luther King Jr. and Gandhi, they took some amazing risks, they had to go through a lot of suffering and hardship . . . there's no way out of that. The point is not to return to violence. You can go out and demonstrate, have a teach-in, you can be involved in plowshares, you can be climbing over the fence into a nuclear testing zone and you can get arrested for that. You have to know in your heart that the violence comes from them. You also have to know that they, The Man, they own all the guns. From the cop out on his beat with a handgun to the hydrogen bomb and everything in between, they own all of them. And The Man will keep inviting you to go down that road, and will you go? How far down that road do you expect to go before he kills you? It is a practical necessity that you do something he does not own. You act nonviolently and he doesn't own that and so he doesn't know how to deal with it. If you ever want to call out the National Guard, the quickest way to do that is to stand out in the middle of the street and shout, "Peace!"

Leslie: You're a traveler.

Utah: Yes, I am.

Leslie: Maybe anyone who really gets in touch with themselves gets in touch with that nomadic urge. How do we reconcile that with stay-at-home parenting?

Utah: Leslie Fielder said that the essence of the American experience is running away from home. Now, dig that. That's what all our songs are about, all our stories. How many people in California are running away from home? You give your kids enough savvy to see what's going on around them so they can avoid sitting around waiting to get hurt. You give them the common sense to be aware and awake, to have a way of approaching people, whether in a railway yard or anywhere, some way of approaching people that lets them know you're not the enemy, you're a friend. That way when they run away they'll know how to deal with it. Not only do I not believe in apron strings, I don't believe in aprons.

Leslie: What about when it's the parents who need to take off?

Utah: [Running away] doesn't mitigate the madness. Sometimes when I took off, it was because I had to, and sometimes it was terribly wrong. There are episodes in my life that I'm not terribly proud of. I was with my kids long enough to give them the analytical tools they need in order to make real choices and real decisions. It had to be by example because they're going to do the same thing. It's not so much the talking, but the doing that is the lesson.

On [my] record [with Ani DiFranco], *Fellow Workers,* it says that the definition of union is: a way to get things done together, which you cannot do alone. Now, all the information about unions and labor that the kids are going to get in school and in books is going to be negative. They're going to walk away from it. I know good union parents who have lived, worked, and fought for unions all their lives, and their kids don't want to know about it. I was talking to a union brother over in Normal, Illinois, and he had the same problem. Then one day he sat down to breakfast with his daughter and she had heard this new record put out by Ani DiFranco on the Righteous Babe label, and all of a sudden she was asking him, "Who was Mother Jones?" He never expected this. He was able to start talking about labor history. It's tremendously exciting, vivid, and useful, and it gives you the tools.

WE'RE FIRED
UP, NOT
GONNA TAKE
IT NO MORE.
THAT'S ME
AND THE
KIDS AND
MY MAMA
AT A
MARCH
BECAUSE THE
PRESIDENT
DID A BOGUS
BILL TO TAKE
MONEY FROM
FAMILIES.
THOSE ARE.
THE PEOPLE
ON THE
STREET
GETTING
TICKETS
FROM
POLICE.

MAiA

Saying No:
How Hunter Convinced Me to Quit Performing Circumcisions

Dr. Barry Brown

ast night, before Hunter and I came upstairs to bed, I called the hospital to schedule a circumcision for the baby whose birth I had attended that morning. I hung up the phone and headed upstairs.

"Daddy," said my three-and-a-half-year-old son, Hunter. "What's a circumcision?"

"It's when someone cuts part of the skin off a baby's penis."

"What part?"

"The foreskin part, the extra that covers up the end. You've probably noticed how your penis still has a little extra skin left, and Daddy's doesn't have any. But Sawyer still has all of his." Sawyer is Hunter's brother, seven months old now.

"Why?"

"Because when I was a baby, my parents thought it was necessary. And when you were a baby, Mommy and I thought it was necessary. But by the time Sawyer was born, we had thought more about it, and we realized it wasn't really necessary."

He thought about it for a minute. "What do you cut it with?"

"Uh . . . a knife. A scalpel blade."

He knows about scalpel blades because I bring them home from the office sometimes and use them to shave calluses off our feet. When he wants to help, we warn him that the blades are sharp and a cut would really hurt.

I don't tell him the part about the metal clamp that comes before the cutting, the clamp that crushes the skin so the cuts won't bleed. It hurts a lot worse than a cut.

"Why?"

"Why what?"

"Why does it hurt?"

"Because it hurts to cut a part of the baby's penis off." But I knew what he was trying to ask. "Are you wondering why I do it?"

I had been asking myself this same question for quite a few months, ever since I reached the verdict that circumcisions are not just unnecessary, but cruel. It started about the time that Hunter was born. I was halfway through residency when he joined us, and my thinking had only advanced as far as to conclude that sons should probably look like their fathers, so they wouldn't suffer confusion. This, plus an ill-examined notion that un-circumcised penises were less aesthetically pleasing, led us to have him circumcised. I was personally unfamiliar with the generously redundant flesh of the foreskin. It seemed to me like a sign of something in us that is beyond primitive, that is simply animal. It defies logic, but my culture had connected this generous redundancy with the uncontrolled male principle. I didn't like the idea of the pain, but my misgivings weren't strong enough to spare Hunter from the clamp and the knife.

Then, as now, I did a lot of reading. I had begun a process of gathering wisdom on birth. This had led pretty naturally into an examination of how American culture denigrates the female principle, especially the beauty and power of the female form. I grasped the destructiveness of the message that the female body is ugly unless squeezed into that modern corset, the model's figure: a false aesthetic, its image inescapable in every commercial medium but almost impossible to find in real life.

The book I was reading argued convincingly that men in America have escaped this cultural corset. The male form is not denigrated, they said; men do not have this abuse visited upon their bodies. But parents were still asking me to circumcise their boys, and I was getting uncomfortable about fixing that precious portion of the boy's body when it wasn't broken.

One day my friend Beth, a midwife I work with, told me about another midwife friend, Linda, who had worked with a community of women who had undergone clitoridectomy followed by infibulation. Each of these women, as a little girl, had had most of her labial tissue cut away, the clitoris as well; what remained was sewn together tightly across her opening. "They looked so strange," Linda said. "All smooth, like Barbie dolls."

These women looked at Linda's body with pity. Viewing her anatomy, they would shake their heads sadly. Yet they possessed a sisterly sympathy toward her and offered to help. "We can make you pretty," they told her. "Do you want us to make you pretty?"

When Paula was pregnant again and we began to dream of a newborn, we talked about what to do if we had another boy. She had detected my change of heart, and though her own aesthetics hadn't changed, she could see my point. By the time Sawyer was born, we didn't have to argue. That just left all the other boys in the world—or at least the ones whose births I attended.

I can talk most mothers out of circumcising their boys. Once they learn it's medically unnecessary, all I have to do is be frank about the pain involved. (I forgot to mention the first part, when the doctor uses a slender metal probe to tear away the network of tiny connections between the foreskin and the glans, which before this are fused together. It's like sliding a paper clip under somebody's fingernail.)

The fathers, if they are involved, are not always as receptive to this argument. If they're actively pro-circumcision, the notion of a little pain does not dissuade them. Last time it was the grandmother who weighed in, after the boy was home. His mother's voice on the phone was heavy with reluctance; it took very little inquiry to discover the source of her reversal. I told her that my duty was to act on her wishes, not her mother's, and that it was clear she herself hadn't changed her mind. "You're right, I haven't," she admitted.

Actually, I've delivered mostly girls since Sawyer was born, and the boys have generally had parents who accept them as they are, either at the onset or after a little education.

But this week I was asked to perform a circumcision, Hunter happened to overhear me scheduling it on the phone, and he asked me a few good, simple questions for which I had no good answers.

Hunter is impressively persistent; he wouldn't relent until I had fully explained. And I gave him the answers that had, so far, kept me from rocking the boat at the clinic where I work.

"Because the parents want it done."

"Why do they want it done?"

"Because they think it's necessary."

"Why?"

"They say it's a tradition in their family."

In this case, this meant that all the men in the father's family were circumcised. I suspected that this tradition had its shallow root in a single generation, uniform in their shorn manhood, products all of the sacred covenant of medical fashion.

Tradition is a concept of little value to a three-year-old. "Why did you have it done on me when I was a baby?"

"Because when you were born, we still thought it was necessary." I didn't want him to think his kind of penis was a mistake. "You know, your penis is fine, even though it's different from Sawyer's. Daddy's is a little different from yours, and yours is a little different from Sawyer's, but they are all fine. Do you like your penis?"

"Yes!" he said, giving a big grin. "Daddy, do you like your penis?"

"Yes, I do. I love my penis."

"Does Sawyer like his penis?"

"He sure acts like it, the way he holds it when we change his diapers. Let's go up to bed now."

As we climbed in next to Paula and Sawyer, who had already drifted off, I realized that Hunter still thought I was going to cut off part of a baby's penis in the morning. He didn't know that he'd convinced me never to do another routine circumcision.

"Hunter," I whispered. "Guess what. I decided I don't want to hurt that baby's penis. You convinced me." I began to anticipate his hearty congratulations. "I'm not going to do that circumcision. They'll have to ask Dr. Talbot instead."

"Will he do it?" Hunter whispered back.

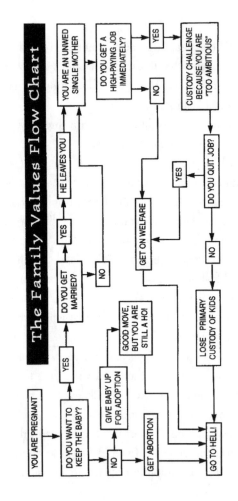

The Family Values Flow Chart

Abortion After Motherhood

Julie Bowles

T hanks to a failed morning-after pill, I found myself sitting with 15 women at the Oakland Women's Choice Clinic a few days before Christmas. Women's Choice schedules first-trimester abortion appointments in groups, where women receive information, education, and counseling in the name of efficiency and empowerment. When I found out they did this, I was skeptical and crabby. After running around with kids all day and doing 10 loads of laundry, why would I want to sit with a group of strangers who probably had no kids, nothing else to worry about, and not a thing in common with me?

But as soon as I sat with these women and listened to them talk, I found a bit of myself where I did not expect to.

"Yeah, I was frying chicken before I came here. I'll probably have to make dinner when I get home," one woman said.

"I need to find a phone; I gotta check on my baby. My sister's probably on the phone. I hate leaving my baby with my sister," another complained.

"I got three kids; I don't need any more. I can't afford them financially or any other way." There were nods of agreement.

193

"I still have Christmas shopping to do. I didn't get anything for my husband yet," another said, reminding us of the holidays.

I was surprised out of my skepticism. We never hear stories of mothers having abortions. But it isn't because we don't have them; it's because we don't talk about it.

I was reminded of a man who once told me, "I don't know any women who have had abortions." "No," I corrected him, "you don't know *of* any women who have had abortions." It seems a subtle distinction, but it is not.

Two weeks later, my Women's Development professor sat reading to us from her doctoral thesis about motherhood after abortion. She was explaining the process women go through after "facing the crisis of abortion," and how women make "more mature decisions as they progress. . . ." Her voice trailed off as I thought of my recent experiences.

These kinds of theories do not allow for the complexities of real lives. They imply that there is a "right way" in which to order a life, and that biology gets more predictable and easier to navigate as we get older, married, wealthier, or more stable.

Why does our culture settle for these easy explanations when they do not fit? Perhaps our images of mothers and our images of women who have abortions are so vastly different that we cannot reconcile the two. Leaving mothers' stories out of the abortion discussion not only denies us our realities but limits the discussion itself.

Statistics tell us that 49 percent of all women who have abortions have also had at least one live birth. Eight and a half percent have had three or more children. These numbers counter the stereotypes and give us a more realistic picture of the women who choose abortion.

Beyond this, however, the statisticians and the theorists leave us hanging. All other abortion data is reported from a women-without-children point of view. Even the Alan Gutmacher Institute, which has conducted the only surveys that ask a woman's reasons for choosing an abortion, leaves out mothers. It has identified three common reasons: "Three-quarters of women say that having a baby would interfere with work, school, or other responsibilities; about two-thirds say they cannot afford to have a child; and one-half say they do not want to have problems in their relationship with their husband or partner."

As stated, these statistics give us no insight into how much already having children factors into the decision to abort. Realistically, these "other responsibilities" must include taking care of a family. Clearly the reason some women "cannot afford to have a child" is because they already have children, and perhaps part of the reason having a baby would "cause problems in their relationship" is because their family is large enough already.

Concerns about money, family size, and quality of life can make some mothers' decisions to have abortions more clear. For me, the decision to not continue my pregnancy did not constitute a crisis, but rather a carefully made decision for myself, my children, my education, and my sanity.

"Some simply do not want to be pregnant or have another baby," says Lynne Vickery, a Renton, Washington, health worker. "For these women, the decision can be very straightforward. The women who make the decision with clarity are not heartless, selfish, inhumane, unwomanly, devoid of 'maternal' instincts, or anything else. I support their clarity as I do the ambivalence of other women."

If we can realize that some women do exercise choice with clarity rather than anguish, we may have to realize that some of the anguish may be socially, religiously, or otherwise institutionally constructed.

In the eyes of the antichoice movement, this would be threatening to publicize. Women could choose abortion without the fear of eternal damnation, insanity, or lifelong regret.

No woman makes the choice to end a pregnancy flippantly. Even if it is not a crisis, abortion is a serious spiritual consideration. These issues can be even more difficult for mothers, who have created life before and know its potential.

When my first child was born, I felt that giving birth was so beautiful, so sacred, that I could never consider having an abortion. I still believe that bringing life into this world is beautiful and sacred, but I have realized this supports arguments for choice rather than contradicting them. It wasn't until I started asking around that I realized my feelings were neither unique nor modern.

One friend said that after going to through two difficult pregnancies, she "felt even more passionately that this is no one's business but my own." This was contrary to her expectation that becoming a mother would make her personally antichoice. Another friend tells the story of her Sicilian grandmother, now 90, who had illegal abortions between each of her four children. After her third abortion, she awoke in the night in a pool of blood. She didn't dare go to the hospital since abortion was illegal and she feared for her safety. But she said her rosary and lived.

Although negative effects of a modern first-trimester abortion are rare, the side effects can include hemorrhaging and infection and may be more likely to occur in mothers, who typically have too much to do. In addition to the usual aftercare instructions, Planned Parenthood usually tells mothers who have had an abortion to "especially take it easy, don't lift children for at least two days, don't stand too long cooking or cleaning, and pay attention to any heavy bleeding or excessive fatigue, but otherwise go about your usual routine."

I laughed when I heard these instructions. How is a mom supposed to follow them? Planned Parenthood also encourages women to enlist the support of partners, relatives, and friends.

As for the spiritual considerations, Zsuzsanna Budapest, author of *The Grandmother of Time,* reminds us, "It is not enough to protect a woman against laws that force her to bear children against her will; it is equally important to take care of her soul after the trauma of the abortion." The ancients believed that fertile women are "constantly accompanied by hundreds of souls, ready to reenter human existence, waiting for a body to slip into." After an abortion, Budapest recommends making an altar for the little soul who got sent back to wait. As she puts it, "Not all souls get bodies, but being without a body is not a tragedy."

Family planning does not end just because we start families. Like every woman who chooses abortion, I made my decision because a new baby would drastically change the course of my life—this time in a direction I could not go.

News Flash

Just Lock 'Em Up

What do you do if two young girls in the midst of a complicated custody battle refuse to follow a court order to visit their father? According to Associate Judge Ludwig Kuhar of Will County, Illinois, you simply lock them up. When the children, ages 8 and 12, refused to travel to North Carolina to visit a father they say is "mentally abusive," Kuhar said he had no other choice but to send the older sister to a juvenile detention center and to confine her younger sister to her house, the *Chicago Tribune* reported in August. Both were released after a day, and the Illinois Appellate Court is examining the matter.

How the God Squad and the Right-Wingers Intend to Mess You and Your Family All Up

Yo Mama

E very visionary knows that child rearing is a high-stakes field. You can raise people to question authority, or you can raise people who will be accustomed to oppression. The human spirit may be naturally rebellious, but as parents and educators, we have immense power to thwart self-confidence, reward "stoicism," and bury that revolutionary spirit until it is all but irretrievable.

Social change cannot take place without familial change. If we envision a patriarchal society, we have to be sure that every woman has a patriarch of her own to keep her in line. If we envision freedom and justice in the world, we have to ensure freedom from abuse and democracy within families.

The "Family Values" campaign was not designed by complete idiots. It was designed by savvy jerks who know full well that the hard-won victories of the civil rights movement and feminism cannot be reversed in a society that celebrates its diversity—particularly its family diversity. The powers that be have tried to fool us into thinking that they really care about things so mundane as who we sleep with, that they've got some kind of concern for our "moral" well-being. In reality, a diverse population is just a heck of a lot harder to control than a patriarchal, white-supremacist one. If women are empowered at home, we aren't going to take any shit at work or on the streets. If kids aren't used to being unquestioningly obedient at home and at school, they're never going to behave as quietly oppressed citizens.

The "Christian" right's political strategy of taking over the school boards before moving on to "higher" government offices was no accident. It wasn't even a "start small" scheme. As Sinead O'Connor said (referring to the supposed potato famine in Ireland that was masterminded not by Mother Nature, as the word "famine" implies, but by the British government), what finally broke the Irish people wasn't starvation "but its use in the controlling of our education." Whoever controls the history books, after all, controls the way we are educated to think about the future. If you can control our societal memory, you're well on your way to controlling our societal destiny.

As Alice Miller documented in her book *For Your Own Good,* it took a long history of authoritarian and abusive child rearing in Germany to create not only Hitler, but the masses who assisted him. She notes that Hitler's henchmen had been so well trained since birth to be obedient that feelings about the atrocities they committed never emerged. At their trials, they claimed they were simply following orders. Adolf Eichmann, for example, could listen to incredibly emotional testimony at his trial in Israel without any visible feelings, and yet he blushed when it was pointed out that he forgot to stand when his verdict was read. Granted, the parallel between the "Christian" right and Nazi Germany (which was, as the Welfare Warriors have pointed out, *full* of two-parent families) might be a bit of a stretch at this point. Still, we're talking about frightening stuff. And it's evidenced in all kinds of social trends and policies.

Take the homeschooling movement. Once dominated by fundamentalist Christians who didn't want their children exposed to a "progressive" education, homeschooling is fast becoming a refuge for lefty families as those same fundamentalists take over the public schools. Hell, *Hip Mama* is even advocating homeschooling at this point.

Or take welfare "reform." If you think for a minute that anyone in Washington really cared about the amount of money Aid to Families with Dependent Children cost us, think again. It was 1 percent of the federal budget, for Christ's sake. But, as we learned with the "potato famine," starving people are a hell of a lot easier to control than even marginally well-nourished ones.

Consider all of the assaults on women's reproductive freedom. Arguments about "baby killing" may help the right-wingers convince their rank and file that abortion is wrong, but since when did our government hold life sacred? (Hello, gajillion-dollar military budget . . . Hello, death penalty.) Even if these boys actually thought that abortion was murder, what's another dead baby in the whole scheme of things? Really. It's about control.

Or consider Growing Families International, the "Christian" parenting curriculum designed to turn naturally revolutionary newborns into obedient "Christians" through abusively rigid feeding schedules and corporal punishment.

And check out the Promise Keepers, an ingenious "Christian"

training program for white guys who can then be sent home to appease and control all of the women, children, and people of color in their families and communities.

I won't go so far as to call this whole thing a conspiracy. It's a little more insidious than that. But it is well orchestrated, it is extremely well funded, and it ain't the least bit accidental.

Okay, so maybe it is a conspiracy.

I Am Your Welfare Reform

Annie Downey

i am a single mother of two children from two different men. I am a hussy, a welfare rider, a burden to everyone and everything. I am anything you want me to be—a faceless number that has no story.

My daughter's father has a job and makes over two grand a month; my son's father owns blue-chip stock in AT&T, Disney, and Campbell's. I call the welfare office, gather old bills, look for daycare, write for my degree project, graduate with my son slung on my hip, breastfeeding.

At the welfare office they tell me to follow one of the caseworkers into a room. It is a small room without windows. The caseworker hands me a packet and a pencil. There is an older woman with graying hair and polyester pants and the same pencil and packet. I glance at her, she looks at me; we are both ashamed. I try hard to fill out the packet correctly, answering all the questions. I am nervous. There are so many questions that near the end I start to get careless. I just want to leave.

I hand the caseworker the packet in an envelope; she asks for my pencil, does not look at me. I exit unnoticed. Five years I've exited unnoticed. I can't imagine how to get a job. I ride the bus home.

After a few weeks a letter arrives assigning me to "Group 3." I don't even read it. I put my son in the stroller and walk to the food closet.

My grandmother calls later to tell me I confuse sex with love. I tell her I am getting a job. She asks what kind. I say, "Any job."

"Oh, Annie," she says. "Don't do that—you have a degree. Wait."

I say, "I can't, Gram. I've got to feed my kids. I have no one to fall back on."

She is silent. I grasp the cord. I know I cannot ask for help.

It is 5 A.M. My alarm wakes my kids up. I try nursing my son back to sleep, but my daughter keeps him up with her questions and fears: "Don't go out without telling me. Who's going to take care of us when you leave? Are you leaving right now? What time is it?" I want to cry. It is still dark and I am exhausted. I've had three hours of sleep. I get ready for work, put some laundry in the washer, make breakfast, set clothes out for the sitter, and make lunches. I carry my son; my daughter follows. They cling to me. They cry when I leave. I see their faces pressed against the porch window, the sitter trying to get them inside.

I slice meat for $5.50 an hour for nine hours a day, five days a week. I barely feed my kids, barely pay my bills.

I struggle against welfare. I struggle against this faceless number I have become. I want my story. I want my life. But without welfare I would have nothing. On welfare I went from a teen mom to a woman with an education. I published two magazines, became an editor and a teacher. Welfare, along with Section 8 housing grants and the Reach Up program, gave my children a life. My daughter loves and does well in school. My son is round, and at 20 months speaks wondrous sentences about the moon and stars. Welfare gave me what was necessary to be a mother.

Still, I cannot claim it. There is too much shame in me. The voices of the grocery lines, open food stamps, disgusted looks, rage of the blue and white collar—the taxpayer voice of *Oprah* panelists. I never buy expensive ice cream in pints. I don't do drugs. I don't own a hot tub. But the voices won't still.

I am one of 11 million who are 1 percent of the federal budget. I am 40 percent of AFDC recipients who are mothers, my children 35 percent. I am 55.6 percent who are white. I am 68 percent of teen mothers who were sexually abused. I am 16 percent who received welfare infrequently as a child. I am $600 a month below the poverty level for a family of three. I am 60 percent of wages of mothers in their first year off welfare. I am a hot political issue. I am 145-65-8563. Group 3.

I have brown hair and eyes. I write prose. My mother has been married and divorced twice. I have never been married. I love Pablo Neruda's poetry and Louise Glück's essays. I love my stepfather but not my real father. My favorite book is *Love in the Time of Cholera* by Gabriel García Márquez. My favorite movie is *The Color Purple.* I miss my son's father. I love jazz. I've always wanted to learn how to ballroom dance. I am not a number. I have a story, a life, a face.

News Flash

Stats to Lie By

Soaring out-of-wedlock births! Skyrocketing teen pregnancy rates! Teenage welfare mothers galore!

Dig: You know how out-of-wedlock birthrates have been soaring over, say, the past 25 years? Common knowledge, right? Well . . . birth certificates do not explicitly state whether the baby's parents are married, so how do the brilliant statisticians figure it out? Simple. They look to see if mom and dad's last names are different. If the names are the same, they count the couple as married; if they're different, they count the couple as unmarried unless they've hyphenated the kid's name, in which case, they are counted as married. Never mind the fact that women often keep their own names after tying the knot, or that hyphenation has no connection to marriage. What it boils down to is that while we know how many female-headed households there are in the country (about 11 million), we have *no idea* how many out-of-wedlock births there are.

Add teen motherhood to the mix. It turns out that each state and federal agency has its own definition of "teenage"—up to age 17, 18, or 19. So all the comparative statistics are useless. Many states with low teen-parenting rates simply aren't counting the 18- and 19-year-olds who make up the vast majority of teen moms.

Finally, the question used to determine whether a welfare mom is also a teen mom is to ask whether she had her first child as a teenager. Never mind if she didn't apply for welfare until she was 40.

Whatever.

Moms Just Wanna Get Paid

Lucinda Marshall

ear Boss,

Let me be blunt: *I deserve a raise.* Actually, I deserve a salary. I have nine years' tenure in my present position. My job involves regular overtime and I am on call 24 hours a day. When I go on vacation, I have to take my work with me. Excepting the intangible benefits (which are the only reason I'm doing this gig in the first place), I receive no salary, no benefits, no retirement fund, no insurance, no sick days, and no stock options.

My work roles require knowledge and skill in many areas and include, but are not limited to, the following:

Chef: Specializing in the creative and quick presentation of PB&J and other nutritious entrées for the discriminating palate.

Transportation Director and Head of Fleet Management: Responsible for delivering clients to school, extracurricular activities, doctors' appointments, and miscellaneous other locations. Frequently required to be in two locations at once. Must keep fleet in usable condition.

Residential Property Manager: Oversee maintenance of residential unit that receives high traffic and heavy-duty use.

Chief Financial Officer: Responsible for keeping outflow less than inflow. Oversee Bookkeeping and Tax Departments.

Triage Nurse: Responsible for dispensing Band-Aids and making preliminary assessments of medical complaints.

Handywoman: Responsible for fixing most everything myself. (My spellchecker informs me that the correct spelling of "handywoman" is "handyman." Responsible for turning said spellchecker off.)

Sanitation Director: Responsible for dustball removal, maintaining the laundry pile at a height of no more than three feet, keeping bathroom mildew farm under control, sandblasting dishes, and disposal of all manner of trash. Have never been cited by the health department.

Activities Coordinator: Have computerized this department, which enables all parties to see the big picture. Must always be prepared for last-minute changes due to weather (and related school closings), illness, ex-spouse, and/or babysitter.

Education Director and Daycare Coordinator: Must enroll children in appropriate educational facilities, fill out paperwork for said facilities, and help at numerous class parties and field trips. When educational facilities are closed, it is my duty to make sure clients are cared for by a responsible party should I not be available (for instance, if I'm "working" or have major surgery scheduled).

Landscape Coordinator: Our company policy and the community by-laws dictate that the grass should not be as high as an elephant's eye. A few live flowers are also considered a nice touch.

Procurement Specialist: This area entails providing all necessary supplies such as food, clothing, and toys for our growing clientele.

My competence in these areas has been a strong contributing factor in the successful growth of this enterprise. I would like to highlight some of our accomplishments to date: My clients are healthy, growing children. They are bright and inquisitive and excel in their schoolwork. They are loving and caring individuals who I believe will be valuable contributors to the growth of this organization.

Realizing that I am in uncharted territory when it comes to asking for a salary, I have done some research, which I would like to share with you. According to *Business Week,* the highest-paid CEO in the United States was paid $102,449,000 in 1996. Further, the average raise for CEOs was 154 percent (factory workers got 3 percent). So, for 1997, we'd be talking about 154 percent of $102,449,000 as a starting point. I would expect the usual perks that befit a person in my position.

If you have any questions about my proposal we can do lunch next week. I'll let you preview my latest PB&J creation.

Sincerely,
Lucinda Marshall, CEO

With Liberals Like These

In mid-January, a nice woman from WNYC, the National Public Radio affiliate in New York, called to ask if I'd like to be a guest on a show called *On the Line*. She had read an article of mine in *In These Times* and wanted me to talk about welfare and teen parenting. I didn't think about it for long. I'd be able to advertise *Hip Mama* free and try out my idea that there is nothing intrinsically wrong with young, single, or poor women having children in the liberal waters of NPR. I agreed. I was actually psyched.

So at 8 A.M. on a Monday I got all my stats in front of me so I wouldn't be caught off guard. I prepared my logical—if radical—arguments in praise of teen moms. I set my daughter up with a bowl of oatmeal and some friends. And I waited with coffee for the call from New York.

The half-hour show began calmly enough. The interviewer asked about *Hip Mama.* He asked what a zine was. He asked about graduate school. He asked about single motherhood, welfare, and domestic violence. And then, of course, he invited listeners to call in. That's when it got ugly.

The first attack came from Joan in New Jersey, who couldn't believe that anyone had given me a college degree, let alone allowed me into grad school. She had kids herself, and a PhD to boot, but she declared, "I couldn't have done it without my husband." She claimed to have put herself through school, something that very few Americans actually do (subsidized student loans, parents' contributions, government grants, and state universities are all subsidized education). "This woman should be taken [I think she's going to say "out and shot"] off welfare," she said. "I've been a liberal all my life, but now I'm at the point where I think the children of single parents should be taken and put into group homes!" *(I gulp down the rest of my coffee.)*

I knew I was putting my butt on the line with my positive ideas about teen parents, but this babe was talking about *all* single parents. And she wasn't the only one. Some guy called from his car phone and, claiming to be a criminal lawyer, said 90 percent of his clients were raised by single mothers (I assume he means his guilty clients). The problem? "No guidance from Dad," he says. *(I try to argue with him for a minute, then realize he ain't an attorney for nothing.)*

By the end of the interview I had been given the following advice: Take a day job; take a night job; spend more time with your kid; don't publish a zine; don't charge money for a subscription; get an income; put your kid in an orphanage; stay in any relationship; and don't go to school. I was also assured that my daughter would be a criminal, that she would suffer because I was single, and that in taking on the role of defending mothers I was "trapping" myself into ignoring the real problems. In short: I, my life, and all my beliefs sucked.

In all fairness to the city, three people did call me after the show to say,

"You go, girl!" and "Not everyone in New York is an ignorant asshole." The ones who agreed with me just couldn't get on the air.

The show was not a major incident. I came out as a welfare mother (kind of like coming out as a communist in the '50s), and four residents of the New York area got a chance to vent their hate. But there were probably mothers listening who are not as self-righteous as I've become. And those angry callers were talking to them, too. I did a pretty good job standing up for us, and I hope I inspired a few people, but I was only one. There were probably mothers listening who took those angry words to heart, who didn't get the three calls afterward and who started the week with a little of their spirit siphoned off by a few ignorant people desperately looking for someone to blame because this country is not the promised land they once dreamed of. *(Surprise, it's Mom's fault!)*

—Ariel

News Flash

Ohio Judge Gets a Clue

Reversing his own order that a man who hit his girlfriend must marry her (and she him), a Hamilton County, Ohio, judge said in July that, on second thought, it was a bad idea.

No shit, your honor.

The original order made national news and stirred a furor among women's organizations and other forms of intelligent life. The municipal court judge, Albert Mestemaker, had ordered a man who pleaded no contest to a domestic violence charge to marry the woman he hit. The judge said he imposed the condition on 26-year-old Scott Hancock because he and his girlfriend said in court that they eventually planned to marry.

In rescinding his order, Mestemaker said in court that it was "ill conceived" and should never have been issued.

Letters to the Editor

Uprising in Nevada?

Dear Hip Mama,

I need advice on how to start an uprising in the state of Nevada. We are one of the worst states in dealing with children's issues. I feel like I should do something, but don't know how to get started. I'm not too politically savvy, though I'm beginning to think that is the key. Thanks,

Sherri Cruz

Las Vegas, Nevada

Get a Job

To the Editor:

If you want to run a magazine, do it, but not while on welfare. Anyone who can write as well as you do is surely capable of supporting herself and a child.

Diane Smith

Northbrook, Illinois

I'm Poor But I'm Happy

Dear Ariel and Company,

EEEK! We just got our fourth issue of Hip Mama for the year. Must be time to renew. Don't want to miss out!

We both (husband and wife—yes, there actually are males who read Hip Mama!) continue to enjoy your special brand of GRRL-ILLA WARFARE! So please keep us on your list for another year's subscription. Don't forget us!

Unfortunately our income has not increased. Wish I could say the same about our expenses! Oh well. Sigh. Looks like another year at the low end of the economic totem pole ("trickle down," my ass!). So please accept our check at the low rate (presumably set up for us "po-folks" in everything but love!).

Lloyd Blailock
Slidell, Louisiana

Absurdly Offensive

Hip Mama:

This is absolutely absurd! Why don't you give real advice to women and keep your "Political Garbage" out of it!

MarJean Morrison
Claremont, California

Editor's Note: Bite me. The parental is political.

After a post–September 11 appearance on CNN in which Ariel noted that our grief was not a call to war and the USA PATRIOT Act was limiting our civil rights in the name of "freedom," a deluge of letters appeared in the email and post office boxes. Here's a selection:

I Seen You on CNN

Ariel Gore,

I seen you on CNN. If you were not born in this country then go back to the country you were born in and see how good you have it. If you were born in this country then leave. It's people like you who have caused this country to be too liberal and allow criminals to run free and commit crimes again and again. If you want a one-way ticket I will buy it for you, just leave and let America be America. FREEDOM IS NOT FREE . . .

Anonymous
Email Land

Response to Hip Mama Guest on CNN Headline News

As far as the PATRIOT Act goes, do not worry about the government tapping your phone or investigating you, they could have done it anyway—but if you are so worried about this then

216

what is it that you are hiding? As a citizen of the United States I begin to wonder, should we be worried about you?

Adam

Email Land

Miss Gore on TV

May I ask, what exactly are you "protesting"? And which war are you protesting? Are you pro–Taliban beatings of women? Are you in favor of other Americans sacrificing their lives so you and your ilk can do nothing but whine?

Greg C.

Email Land

This Is for Ariel Gore

If you truly feel your civil rights are being violated, may I suggest you find another country to live in. I suggest you enlist in any of the services under the Department of Defense and serve on some remote location fighting for the rights of those American citizens that appreciate what we stand for. You are a pathetic citizen. I am insulted that you call yourself an American.

Michael Culler

Email Land

So Naïve

Dear Ms. Gore,

My dear girl, you are so nieve [sic]. I shudder to think that you are in such an influential position, and you use it so worthlessly. Do you think you'd be more comfortable in a burqa?

A concerned American father and grandfather

Email Land

Ariel,

I just watched your interview on CNN and I want to congratulate you on bringing up all the points that you did and having the courage to state your opinion. Seeing someone express the concern (if not outrage) about the current events on the news felt like a breath of fresh air. I had been wondering where the voices of the young people in this country were and whether anyone realized what exactly is taking place right now. It was great to see someone speak up in the time when everyone around seems to have lost touch with reality and just blindly parrots what is being dictated by the current self-exalted government.

Tatiana

Email Land

Ariel,

It was brave of you to speak your mind. I thought it was hilarious that one of those emailers said you fit the terrorist profile. Why, sir, is it the eyebrow pencil?

It's also interesting to peer into the mindset of the people who wrote the emails—i.e. the belief that freedom is something bestowed upon people by beneficent governments, military employment is about protecting freedom and has nothing to do with protecting political and economic agendas of imperialist powers, only American deaths from bombs really hurt, and anyone who doesn't agree with all this must emigrate immediately. I don't think these people represent a majority opinion but unfortunately I do think the future of the country belongs to them and to their level of brainlessness, leading to eventual overt dictatorship, as we've discussed. And when the president comes on TV to say he's suspended the Constitution altogether, he'll say it's for national security, and freedom, and democracy, and the networks will back him up with dazzling flag graphics.

Jeff
Berkeley, California

Faith and Irreverence:
UnVirgin Births

Sunday	Monday	Tuesday	Wednesday
			1 Take kid to martial arts. Listen to Resident Bush spewing about "evil" on TV.
5 Paint house. Move. Throw back out. Have party. Pass out.	**6** Take kid to martial arts. Up all night planning armed insurrection.	**7** Cancel therapy. Make fool of self & others on NPR.	**8** Take kid to martial arts. Provoke angry patriots on CNN. Worry about being un-American.
12 Kid buys all pink clothes, gets her hair feathered. Bite tongue.	**13** Take kid to martial arts. Then cheerleading. Bite harder.	**14** Cancel therapy. Get teaching job at high school.	**15** Take kid to martial arts. Teach Bukowski to high schoolers.
19 Fly to Mexico City & bus 12 hours to visit parents.	**20** Sleep in "servants' quarters." Go see pre-Columbian ruins.	**21** Long-distance call to cancel therapy. Mom breaks out mezcal.	**22** Try & remember Spanish. Keep getting it confused with Italian.
26 Puke for six hours on bus back to parents' house.	**27** Cancel therapy. Fly home. Immigration doesn't think kid is mine.	**28** Finally make it home to fire off hundreds of angry emails to White House.	**29** Sister finds work as ghostbuster in our childhood neighborhood.

Thursday	Friday	Saturday
2 Sick in bed. Read Emma Goldman autobiographies.	**3** Fire off nasty emails to politicians. Feel slightly better.	**4** See the sun in Portland. Worry when this results in mild headache.
9 Keep eyes peeled for suspicious people getting into crop-dusters.	**10** Try & inseminate lover at biker bar.	**11** Take a dozen preteens to see Britney Spears movie. Worry after enjoying it.
16 Cancel therapy. Student asks if I want to buy pot. "Hello?! I'm your teacher!"	**17** Catch Republicans dumping ballots in bay.	**18** Get arrested for "illegally catching Republicans dumping ballots."
23 Kids want Third World hottie outfits. Drink margaritas with Grandma.	**24** Take bus to coast. 11 hours for supposedly 100-mile trip.	**25** Settle into hammock for day. Swat mosquitoes.
30 Kid wins medals at martial arts championship. So don't mess with us!		

yo mama's daybook

Road Revelations

Nanci Olesen

I miss who I was in the driver's seat, in the middle of Colorado in the middle of the night, my children scrunched in the back sleeping, my spouse snoring in an awkward position next to me. I remembered things I hadn't thought of for a long time as I wound over the mountain passes. I drank really bad coffee, and even let it get cold, and continued to drink it, cold and bad. Then I felt my eyes get fuzzy, and I had to keep myself awake by singing all of the *Tapestry* album. Then I sang everything I could think of. I planned my funeral. I tried to remember every phone number of every friend in grade school.

Then I drifted through thoughts of old boyfriends, through other late-night trips. I talked to my brother in my head for a long time and told him everything he needed to know about me. I changed our whole relationship in my head and felt a delightful peace wash over me. I saw eyes of deer flash in the headlights and strange lumps—huge rocks that looked like bears. When dawn came and my mouth felt like the inside of a gym shoe and our children rustled under their sweaty covers and looked out to see the orange sky and the desert rocks of Utah, we stopped at a rest stop and washed our faces and brushed our teeth and stretched our bodies in the early morning sun. We found a place to eat breakfast and after the hash browns and the eggs and more really bad coffee, I felt like I was falling into sleep faster than I ever had. I slept all the way to the Bryce Canyon entrance while my husband drove and the children argued and drew with markers on their scribble pads and spilled their juice.

Then we stumbled out of our van and walked to the edge of the canyon and the sun was hot and the sky was blue and we were so far from home and the children were more beautiful than I had ever seen them and we ate raisins and read about how the canyon was formed and filled our water bottles at the drinking fountain and I was so incredibly happy. I miss who I was that day. (August 1999)

Something about the night, the late winter night, the way the kids are so excited to sleep in the car . . . jammies on at 7 P.M. while I load up all our belongings from a three-day trip to Grandma and Grandpa's. They barely fit, lying down in the back of the small station wagon, and they are so excited and squirmy and giggly that I don't even try to interrupt them with "Okay, it's time to go to sleep . . ." But as the trip begins, the giggly excitement turns to tiredness, impatience, and the predictable nit-picking until they are in tears, shouting at each other about what each person did and who started it. For some reason I am just listening, as if to a soundtrack . . . calmly steering the car through the twilight on a small northern Wisconsin highway. I suddenly miss my own brother so much I can hardly stand it. I hear the arguments and it sounds as though one of the voices is mine, 30 years ago, probably on the same damn road. "There's no room for my leg!" I imagine my mom trying to calm us down, exasperated at the end of a long day . . . then I hear my current voice, which sounds so much like my mother's voice: "You guys, I

want to hear no more talking. Heads on your pillows. Just calm down."
This lasts for maybe one mile, then someone else commits an outrage
and it all begins again. I stop the car outside Wayne's Restaurant and
Truck Stop and get everyone all organized again. Covers on straight, pillows the right way. And off into the night. This time it works, and they
are asleep in eight or nine miles. I look back at them at a four-way stop
and see their damp little foreheads, scrunched in deep sleep, each child
lying carelessly on another, and they are they are they are—my children . . .
my sweet fleeting children who will drive me out of my mind every day.
My children whom I fret over and laugh about and coerce into jackets
and carry and heave around. I drive on in silence, thinking, feeling the
fleetingness of it . . . the way time just plows on, and I weep and laugh
and drive. I write letters in my head to my brother and have imaginary
conversations, picturing us finally resolving our difference and becoming
best friends. I plan my next few days—I imagine the phone messages
that are waiting for me . . . the email messages that will certainly lead to
more opportunities. I drive and drive to my own house and unlock my
own door and see the carefully kept bachelorness of my partner's three-
day stay alone. I can feel how much he missed us and how wonderful it
was for him to sleep in the morning without our big loud kids . . . then I
lift each one out of the scrunched back seat and carry each one to his or
her bed, in order of youngest to oldest. I cover each one gently and kiss
each one and run to write it down . . . write it down . . . what? . . . that
I love them? That I can't believe I have three kids? That I want to see
my brother? That I love my parents? That we need to get a bigger car?
Yes. All of the above. (3:48 A.M., 2000)

The Lion Who Ate Pancakes + Noodles

Story by Nilsa Brady   illustrated by Jill Brady

Once a lion went out for pancakes.

When he got home, his house was a river.

Then he went back to the restaurant and ate noodles.

When he got back his house was his house again.

Then he went back to the restaurant and ate pancakes.

When he got home his house was a Pancake.

Hip Mama Asks: Got Faith?

F aith. It makes folks do some funky things. (Why not: shave your head and chant at the airport; put a Jesus fish on your car; have a baby; move to Jonestown; be kind to strangers; kill people; re- fuse medical care . . .) But how many of us can say that spirit has never touched our lives? Do you pray? To whom? Do you leave sacrifices on altars? Worship in forest clearings? Give thanks? Is this moment a result of your destiny or your choices? Is there a difference? These are, per- haps, some of the last personal questions. But *Hip Mama* asked. . . .

Zen Mary

My faith resurfaced six months back when my son was born with tran- sient tachypnea and I was told that he had a moderate chance for sur- vival. I prayed and prayed, and then prayed some more.

His father spent the nights he was in the NICU beside him (I was busy recovering from stitches, OW!) until the nurses kicked him out, when he'd rejoin me and we'd each do our own version of prayer (Ryk sits Za- Zen). The day came when he was reunited with us in a "rooming-in" set- ting for three days and then home—I never thanked Mary more for any- thing in my life. My little one is now, and ever shall be, a strong and wise little man-child. I did not put all my eggs in the prayer basket, but it certainly helped me when I could've gotten hysterical over the whole thing.

Oh, and, incidentally, I feel that in times of maternal crises and even when things are going swimmingly, Mary is the one to call on. After all, she was the mother of an amazing man (a prophet and savior, as some see him). I think he was way ahead of his time, going around helping those in need when he was dirt-poor himself.

So, yes, I do have faith and do also feel that the God of some is not necessarily the God of all. And prayer can be just a mantra or a personal belief. We all get our higher power from somewhere.

—Mamarama

Eternal Oneness and Stained Glass

I believe in eternal oneness, the Gaia Hypothesis, majik spells, and witchy coincidences. Even my guardian angel. Religion/faith has become of increasing concern to my daughter and me as we get older. It all started when, at 20 months, the girl became strangely but adamantly obsessed with stained-glass windows. We entered every church within a five-mile radius and studied the colored light on the floor, on the pews, on the walls. We studied the pictures depicted in the colored glass: "Honey, there are two men and a sun and a cup . . ." Each time, while I explained to her and she explained to me the superficial configuration of the figures, I would try to analyze a mystery. Who were the figures really? What story was I seeing? What did it mean? I would struggle with my failing memory of my own childhood faith—is that Jeremiah? Who was Jeremiah? Or Jeremy, was it? How will I know if that's him? I would struggle with faiths I had never known, trying to access a memory or a mystery deeper than my own. I felt that people who knew those stories, the stories depicted carefully in bits of colored glass, were lucky. Lucky to believe in something, lucky to know a special little story. Selective. Selected.

So we went to the Unitarian church one Sunday morning. They greeted me and asked what I was there for.

I said, "You can believe anything here."

They said, "Well, not anything." We spent the hour in the basement preschool.

But I think I understand the nature of the universe, the meaning of life, the ultimate truth. It is "Energy cannot be created or destroyed." It is "What you do to the planet you do to yourself." It is "God is everywhere," and decomposing and a plant's life cycle. It is a vision of the earth as one living, breathing, mortal organism. Each one of us is a bit of nature, biology, God.

But the light sure looks neat slanted red and yellow and green through a stained-glass window.

—Jillian Brady

Rebel Without a Deity

I'd love to have a faith in some kind of deity, but I can't. I was born a natural rebel; I've always chafed against authority, so it goes without saying the whole Bible thing does not work for me. I vacillate between the Camus universe, totally random and meaningless, and a happier universe that is an amalgam of the wisdom of mysticism, nature, and art. When I read an incredible piece of poetry, when I write, when I hear inspired music, when I look at my sleeping daughter's face, I believe in beauty and divinity. When I think about the people I love and who surround me, the history, the laughter, the hard times, I believe in soul mates. I believe in destiny. I believe in ghosts. I believe that everyone has a calling. When

I'm in my Camus mode I get so overwhelmed when I think about the human suffering and misery in the world, I could cry. Where is the divinity? In the kabbalah, the explanation for the existence of evil and sorrow in our world is that God once existed as a golden energy above us all but has been shattered, and the golden shards surround us here on earth. Every time we do something with goodness and joy and love, we lift up a golden shard to the sky and replace God, piece by piece. I love that. I've stumbled between telling my children that when we die, we become blue sparks of energy and go back to the earth around us, and telling them that we go to heaven. The idea of pearly gates and harps and angels has somehow been fed to them by our society, and I don't worry about it too much. That's the only way they can process death, I suppose.

—Julie Gray

Yoruban-based Afro-Cuban

I am definitely a faith-observing person. Yoruban-based Afro-Cuban religion. I've always been spiritual, but with this religion I have found a support system that never fails me and never goes away. I have come to realize that, as my elders say, all of my prayers are answered; it's just that sometimes the answer is *No!*

Three things propelled me to look for an organized religion. One was having my daughters, ages six and nine; the second was losing my mother to cancer; and the third was being post–Saturn return! All of these events have encouraged and compelled me to find a deeper meaning for why the hell I am here and why the hell I am who I am.

Faith means I can let my daughters even leave the house. Faith makes it possible to sometimes fail miserably as a mother but know that I also do a whole lot just right.

Just being out in the world is so amazing sometimes.

In my religion all of our "angels" have forces in nature or natural occurrences attributed to their personalities. When I see a rainbow, I know that Yemoja is wishing me well and reminding me that she is always there for me. When a homeless man walking by talking to himself turns to smile at me, I do not turn away. I smile and say hi because I know that Esu reminds me to stay in balance and never take things for granted. I am so happy to be able to pass some of that wonder along to my girls. May they always find faith to help them glide gracefully through life.

—Inga Aaron

Red-Diaper Atheist

I was born and raised red-diaper atheist and continue to call myself this. If I had to pick a "faith" I would choose Taoism. I suppose it is more of a philosophy, but it is deeply spiritual. My daughter is three and has been exposed to my beliefs as well as those of her extended family. Her father is Filipino Catholic, and very open-minded. When I confront him on some of the unsavory parts of the Bible, he says, "It's just a book." Much as he is very low-key about the rules of Catholicism, he is overwhelmed with guilt if he misses church for more than a couple weeks. While I don't believe in the metaphysical parts of Catholicism, I do strongly identify with the revolutionary, egalitarian, and democratic aspects of Jesus's teaching.

My daughter enjoys going to church with my husband, especially lighting the candles. She asks me why I don't pray. I answer, Because I think if you want something you have to work for it yourself, but sometimes I think it feels good to wish for something really hard. She asks us, Why did they nail Jesus to the cross? We answer that Jesus wanted them to share but they didn't want to, so they nailed him to the cross.

I am happy to have Catholicism to use as a teaching tool of morals and ethics as long as we don't emphasize the toxic parts of it. Taoism is just too abstract for a three-year-old.

—Valentina

Rebel Without a Deity #2
All my life I made a full-time job out of rebelling against the religion I inherited. One thing I overlooked while I was busy trying to be a bad-ass phony intellectual is that, in addition to oppressive dogma, religion can also pass on culture and expose kids to spirituality. However, I'm still fairly noncommittal at this point.

—Vanessa Stefanelli

God of Sobriety
When I got sober, I made my relationship with god the center of my life. I had tried to get sober for 10 years, so when I finally "got it," I got it in a big way. The pink cloud period lasted about three years and then I got pregnant. David and I decided to go for the whole thing so we got married when I was four months pregnant. I cried. I cried from the moment I found out I was pregnant through the whole first year of my son's life. I cried out of sheer gratitude. Gratitude that I was sober, alive, and had this most beautiful baby and this man who wore daddyhood like a perfect-fitting Armani suit. There must be a god, I would think, because my life is too good to be true. I've been lucky. All the shitty things in my life happened between the ages of 12 and 29. I still pray, while in the shower, doing the dishes, or changing a diaper. My prayers are usually, "Thanks, god, for this really cool life." I try to get Cooper to say, "Thanks god," too. When we talk about god, we usually refer to god as

she or *her*. Cooper has been blessed with a very feminist, hip grandma who has influenced me, too.

—Holly Cardone Shaw

Rebel Without a Deity #3

I was born into a devoutly Roman Catholic family and educated in parochial schools from first grade through college. Therefore, all of my knowledge/decisions about God, goodness, lust, sex, birth control, and which gender could be correctly identified as the true representatives of Jesus and which could be called "vessels of sin" were preordained by a hierarchy of single, celibate men. These beliefs were already seriously frayed by the time I became a mother, but the last tethers of my faith gave way with the arrival of my second son, born 18 months after his brother. I was 27, with nearly a quarter-century of reproductive years ahead of me, and had to ask: Did I want to have another child every 18 months? The concept of birth control took on new meaning for me. And although it would be some time before lust reappeared—mere sleep was far more seductive when living with infants and toddlers—when it did, sex without fear of further reproduction brought me closer to heaven than anything I have known so far.

This led to many, many other questions about how much wisdom I could depend on from a hierarchy that, for 2,000 years, has not included one parent, let alone one woman . . . and whose chief female inspiration was a virgin mother. Did I want my sons to regard any woman who did not aspire to this goal as a "vessel of sin?" No.

We were not a religiously organized family and had only a tentative attachment to dogma. But both of my sons, attracted by the solidarity of Christian friends, periodically joined religious congregations (in addition to their soccer teams) and experimented with church membership and youth groups. Especially as teens, they wanted to belong to a community of believers. When they invited me to join them for a service or a meeting, I did. If I couldn't share their belief in the faith of the moment, I could always be moved—sometimes awed—by the sincerity of their quest.

Now aged 23 and 25, they are deeply familiar with God talk in several languages: their grandmother's Roman Catholicism, their paternal grandparents' Missouri Synod Lutheran faith, their beloved uncle's Zen practice, and their secular mother's near-death experience. I think it would be safe to say that they have, by now, witnessed all manner of fractious human beings trying to be more divine, with greater or lesser grace. Their religious beliefs, I would guess, are still under construction.

So I don't know what you'd call my faith—I have a deep affinity with people who care about others as much as themselves, despite heresies about "personal responsibility" and "three strikes and you're out." I feel lucky to have been inspired by some of the great prophets of my day, but I tended to find them more often at ERA rallies and civil rights marches than at pulpits. But if I didn't suspend my disbelief in the daily headlines and put pure faith in the possibility of redemption, I wouldn't get up every morning.

As for the Teletubbies and Mr. Falwell, I do not believe in the death penalty, even for televangelists who solicit money in the name of God. But if there is a hell, and God is as wrathful as most of them suggest, they'd be wise to heavily invest in asbestos.

—Mary Kay Blakely

The Spirituality of Cleaning

Maria Doss

This is not going to be a discussion about who is supposed to clean or how to talk ourselves into cleaning or why women get stuck doing most of the cleaning or how to manipulate those you share your habitat with into doing more of the cleaning.

This is an opinion, bathed in light cast by the movie *Household Saints* by Nancy Savoca.

There is spirituality in cleaning.

I know little about religion and my views on spirituality are a work in progress at best, but I know what I know. I know what I feel to be true. Speaking truth purges the soul of the mucky buildup of day-to-day living. So I feel it's my duty.

Cleanliness is not next to godliness, unless you view the world through what it means to god. And I do not. But I do find myself thinking quite often about spirituality. And lately, about cleaning.

I've heard that the Zen approach to housework is to find peace and contentment in necessary tasks.

Find it where you can.

But take the outlook of a saint (yes, a real saint) and you have an actual vendetta to clean, a mission to scrub, a calling to take pleasure in doing the "little things" for god. That's what happened in *Household Saints*. Now, I'm not a religious person. But something was triggered in me. It was not a conversion; it was more like a validation.

Isn't there something innately spiritual about cleaning? Cleansing your home—cleansing the environment of your soul. Refreshment, purity, sanctity?

What is it that drives some of us to enjoy the tasks of housework? And why some times more than others? Why do some women say they go into great cleaning frenzies just before their periods? The rising female power that calls out for us to take care. Scrub the tub and soak in its smooth, shiny shell.

This is not an essentialist position.

But why has cleaning been co-opted as a duty, a drudgery, something done only for those around us and rarely for ourselves? What is it that makes a three-year-old child pick up her toys with no prompting and place them in the toy box, or ask for the spray bottle and rag to wash the windows? You could never ask a three-year-old to wash the windows, but let him find it himself and he may love it.

The simple act of wiping away dirt.

I've heard that science has replaced religion and become the universal belief system. Where does that leave the domestic scientist but closer to the essence of humanity?

This is not a woman's destiny.

Sometimes I try to recapture that sense of satisfaction I felt as a child surrendering myself to dusting and making the surfaces in my home shine. The pleasure in doing little things. The simple act.

All that said, I don't think there is anything inherent about the drive to clean. There is only what I know to be a profound joy in a clean space for myself. A spiritual well being. Call it Zen. Call it closer to god. Call it what you want. I'll call it peace.

It's like when all the laundry is done. You know?

News Flash

PBS Gives Voice to New Age Demons

A fundamentalist minister in North Carolina has declared that Barney the dinosaur is, in fact, a "New Age demon who promotes homosexuality."

According to Rev. Joseph R. Chambers of the Paw Creek Ministries in Charlotte, legions of blanket-huggers across the fruited plain are being indoctrinated by a purple dinosaur whose message is plainly antithetical to God's good word. Barney is the latest manifestation of the fact that "America is under siege from the powers of darkness," Chambers warned.

A Patron Saint of Housewives

By Sin Derella

Forget Harriet Nelson and June Cleaver. If there's a 1950s housewife who deserves sainthood, it's Erma Bombeck.

At 37 she was "too old for a paper route, too young for social security, and too tired for an affair." So the fabulous comedian and more-fabulous housewife set out to write a humor column. In 32 years, Erma wrote her way onto the pages of 900 newspapers around the country, authored 11 best-selling books (including *Family: The Ties That Bind . . . And Gag!*), and appeared on ABC's *Good Morning America* for nearly a dozen years—all to share with the world the aggravation (and joys) of living with a dude with a serious attachment to the remote control and washing machines that routinely ate one sock out of each pair.

Among her 10 commandments, Erma urged: "Never have more children than you have car windows," "Never lend your car to someone to whom you have given birth," and "Given the choice between marrying the man of your dreams and a plumber, choose the latter. Men who can fix your toilet on Sundays are hard to come by."

Okay, so Erma wasn't exactly a feminist. In fact, she completely missed the point. "When did a woman selling orange slices in the dime store become more impressive than a woman who did a darned good job raising three kids?" she once wrote on the subject.

But for a woman with the luminous heart of a 1950s housewife, this isn't a sin that should disqualify her from eternal devotion.

In early April 1996, at the age of 69, Erma died of complications after a kidney transplant. And although it's easy to see the sadness in her passing, we prefer to look at it as the first step toward sainthood.

According to a reliable Catholic source, the road to divinity is a long one, but death is where it all begins. After death, the potential saint has to be nominated by some impressive institution or individual—"a government or bishop or something." While our source didn't mention "a zine," we think *Hip Mama*'s formidable stature will suffice. After this nomination, we wait for the Vatican's "Bureau of Sainthood" (formerly known as "The Inquisition") to do a background check verifying Erma's theological and moral correctness. Presuming she checks out as venerable, the case will be set aside.

That's where you come in.

According to our source, the folks at the Bureau of Sainthood then wait for Erma to become the "subject of devotional practice" and for this practice to result in a "groundswell of miracles."

Simply put, we think every *Hip Mama* reader should cut out the Erma image, affix it to a seven-day candle, and humbly pray like hell. When the miracles begin—such as the resurrection of missing socks, or the healing of the couch potato, or the second coming of the plumber—we all write to the Vatican and attest to Erma's power and holiness.

Saint Erma Bombeck. A patron saint of housewives. Why not?

News Flash

Sentences That Have Actually Appeared in Church Bulletins

(and you thought we needed a proofreader!)

This afternoon there will be a baptismal in the South and North ends of the church. Children will be baptized at both ends.

Tuesday at 4 P.M. there will be an ice cream social. All ladies giving milk, please come early.

Thursday at 5 P.M. there will be a meeting of the Little Mothers club. All wishing to become little mothers will please meet the minister in his study.

This being Easter Sunday, we will ask Mrs. Johnson to come forward and lay an egg on the altar.

The ladies of the church have cast off clothing of every kind and they may be seen in the church basement on Friday afternoon.

This evening at 7 P.M. there will be a hymn sing in the park across from the church. Bring a blanket and come prepared to sin.

Looking for Answers: The Virgin Birth

Laura Allen Sandage

I'm going to say right at the outset that I was not raised a Christian, which may be why no one has ever explained these things to me. But I've got a lot of questions about this virgin birth business.

First there's the Annunciation, where the whole thing got started. It seems a little far-fetched, if you ask me. I mean, if some guy named Gabriel came up to me and said, "the Big Man wants you to have his baby," I'd be more likely to call him a pimp than an angel. It's really pretty surprising that those old-fashioned patriarchs went along with her story. In the Middle Ages and Renaissance, women who had sex with spirit beings in their dreams were burned at the stake. But Mary announces, "I was visited by an angel and I'm giving birth to a savior virginally" (maybe she meant to say "vaginally"), and everyone says, "Okay, fine. We'll come bearing gifts in nine months."

Now, how much do we really know about sex education in biblical Galilee? How do we determine Mary's sexual literacy? Maybe Gabriel was some weirdo down the street who liked to dress up in flowing clothes and go prowling at night. Maybe Mary thought if this "angel" didn't kiss her, she was still a virgin. Let's face it, if you can think of a line, some guy somewhere has used it to try to get a woman into bed. "I'm an angel. You will have a virgin birth and your child will be the Messiah" is not any more outrageous than a few lines I've heard.

The story is too familiar. When the angel shows up, flattering her with his "blessed art thou among women" routine, Mary is at first "troubled, . . . and cast in her mind what manner of salutation this should be." But by the time the flashy smooth talker finishes with her, she can't wait to tell her girlfriend Elizabeth, "He that is mighty hath done to me great things; and holy is His name." I can remember when I thought that way, when I went around writing "his name" on every binder and desktop, and just couldn't wait for the next round of "great things" to be done unto me.

But even if I buy the whole angel bit and assume Mary was a pregnant virgin (but different from the heavy-petting kind I've read about in cautionary Ann Landers columns), I'm still left with a few concerns, perhaps the kind of concerns only a woman would have. I can still remember the pain I felt the first few times I had sex, and I just hate to think of poor little Mary being stretched open from the inside by the Savior's head. A head is just a little bigger than most girls would like their first time out. Very, very uncomfortable. Inhumane, I would even say, on the part of the Heavenly Father. Why couldn't He pick a mother of six? She'd be more experienced, have an easier birth, and still have kids to keep her company in her old age, after the Crucifixion.

One more technicality: I can't help wondering, what did they do with the holy placenta? And His sacred umbilical cord? Think of how much those things would be worth today if someone had had the foresight to tuck them away. They already knew from the angel and the star and everything that this was the Christ child. They should have been extra careful. Or His little foreskin, severed eight days later—what happened to it?

I know this is all very irreverent, maybe even irrelevant, but, like I said, I wasn't raised Christian, so I'm really curious. I'm just one of those people who has to know all the gory details before I can be satisfied that a story is for real.

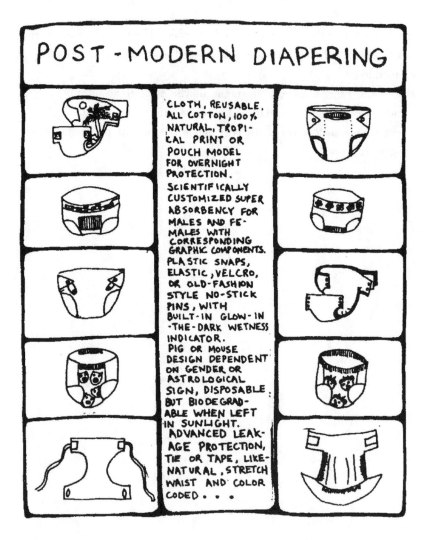

POST-MODERN DIAPERING

CLOTH, REUSABLE. ALL COTTON, 100% NATURAL, TROPICAL PRINT OR POUCH MODEL FOR OVERNIGHT PROTECTION.
SCIENTIFICALLY CUSTOMIZED SUPER ABSORBENCY FOR MALES AND FEMALES WITH CORRESPONDING GRAPHIC COMPONENTS.
PLASTIC SNAPS, ELASTIC, VELCRO, OR OLD-FASHION STYLE NO-STICK PINS, WITH BUILT-IN GLOW-IN-THE-DARK WETNESS INDICATOR.
PIG OR MOUSE DESIGN DEPENDENT ON GENDER OR ASTROLOGICAL SIGN, DISPOSABLE BUT BIODEGRADABLE WHEN LEFT IN SUNLIGHT.
ADVANCED LEAKAGE PROTECTION, TIE OR TAPE, LIKE-NATURAL, STRETCH WAIST AND COLOR CODED . . .

A Close Encounter:
Kimberly Bright Interviews Nina Hagen

S inger, songwriter, musician, and actress Nina Hagen has been one of the most influential women in punk for over 20 years. Americans probably saw Nina for the first time on *The Tonight Show* or MTV in the early 1980s, with her stylish, colorful clothes, hair, and makeup and exuberant personality. Europeans might remember the fuss she caused on an Austrian talk show by demonstrating female masturbation techniques.

Nina was born in East Berlin in 1955 to a well-known German theatrical couple—Eva-Marie, a famous actor, and Hans Hagen, a scriptwriter. Her parents broke up when she was two. The Berlin Wall went up when she was six. She left school before the end of 10th grade, and, upon being denied admission to the state acting school at 17, she went to Poland and joined her first band. At 19, she was named best newcomer singer of the year at a singing contest in Karl-Marx-Stadt and starred in her first movie, *ABC der Liebe*.

Her mother's companion and Nina's foster father, Wolf Bierman, a protest singer and songwriter, so enraged authorities that he was expelled from East Germany in 1976. Nina and her mother followed him into exile. She went to London in 1977, where she jumped into the punk and reggae scene, befriending, among others, the legendary Slits and forming the Nina Hagen Band. With her vast emotional vocal range and charismatic presence, she won over an international devoted cult following. She set out on a solo career in 1980.

It was while writing the material for her legendary first solo album, *NunSexMonkRock,* that Nina became pregnant with her daughter, Cosma Shiva, by musician Ferdinand Karmelk. For two decades she has balanced motherhood and work, continuing her acting, singing, recording, performing, her own TV talk show *(Nina's Welt),* and political/ social activism (the antiapartheid movement, animal rights, feminism, hospice work, and fundraising in India). For most of that time she has lived all over the world as a single mother.

Now 46, she is the mother of two children: actress Cosma Shiva, age 21, and Otis, 12, son of Franck Chevalier, a music manager. She has a long-standing interest in Eastern mysticism, is a student of the Yogi Babaji, and practices Bhakti-Yoga (union with God through love). Her album *The Return of the Mother* was released in 2001, and she has recently written a song called "United Women of the World," celebrating mothers.

She talked to me from her home in Berlin in between concert performances.

Kimberly: What were your pregnancy and birth experiences like?

Nina: Since many years I was longing for a baby. Back in my hometown of East Berlin, behind the Iron Curtain, I was only 19; many of my girl-friends had a baby already. I was pregnant. I was very excited, but in the third or fourth month I started having real big tummy pains. The doctor said, "Appendix!" so I was pregnant and they had to remove my appendix. The anesthesia was terrible. I remember I could hear the operating doctors talk about my famous mother while they were cutting and stitching, and then I felt PAIN, PAIN, PAIN. The anesthesia was too weak to numb my pain, but still so strong that I could not scream or even only tell [them] "Stop! I can feel the pain!" My pregnancy was still intact after the operation, but only three weeks later I had bleeding. The doctor put me in a hospital bed and said that I had to lie down as long as possible. Anyway, one day my bleeding stopped. I went to the hospital bathroom by myself but when I came back the bleeding had started stronger than ever. So the doctors explained to me that the baby is too small to live if we induce birth now, and they said that the baby might be dead already. And so they induced "crampmakers." My cramps became so strong, and without any intermission, that I screamed. My auntie Ingrid, my mom's sister, worked at this hospital as a nurse. She was there with me, comforting me. She told the doctor that my "drop" is too strong. Anyway, finally I had the urge to press and I was very sad. I did not dare to look at the baby. It must have been very, very small. It did not hurt coming out. I was crying for days and nights. My sweet girlfriend Tine Biermann came to me with her baby boy Benjamin, and I could cuddle with him! I prayed to God and thanked Him that my baby was not coming into our world, because it might have been sick. I prayed that one day soon, I would be able to have a healthy baby.

And when I was 26 I became pregnant with my first child, Cosma Shiva. The pregnancy was very nice. I was so happy at all times, read great books about spirituality, divinity, and pregnancy. First, when I found out that I was pregnant I started having the "pregnancy sickness" not only in the morning. It was LABOR already! I was on tour and had to sing every night! I felt so sick onstage. I bought myself a hospital nurse outfit and a little children's toy carriage with fake hospital stuff on it. Being dressed like that, it made it easier for me to act out my sickness. Even so, I felt really bad. Sometimes I had to run off the stage and vomit quickly, took a mouthwash, and back to the microphone. I managed to make people laugh! I did not like my favorite soap anymore. I could not understand how I could ever stand the smoke of cigarettes. (I was a smoker before.) I stayed clean for six years to follow.

I had a very special encounter of the third kind. It was when I was pregnant in the fourth month; we had just been back from our European tour and moved into a very nice holiday house directly on Malibu Beach in the world-famous Colony, Bob Dylan and Barbra Streisand being neighbors (never saw them). One evening after saying goodnight to my mom, who was just visiting and staying in one of the downstairs bedrooms, my girlfriend Sascha (sleeping in the winter garden), and my bass player Karl Rucker and my manager Juliana Grigorova, who were staying at the guesthouse, I went upstairs to my bedroom, went for a last pee, brushed teeth, and went to the windows. I closed the curtains on the huge window (the sun always comes out very early, and I thought, Better close it, then I can sleep longer), then I went to bed and fell asleep. I wake up in the middle of the night and go to the window. I open the curtains, and I'm standing in awe, for I see a big lightship hovering peacefully in the black night sky, beaming out one fluorescent and magnificent color light after the other. I had only one thought left in my head: "Oh God, am I happy!" And a little impulse thought was: "Oh, shit . . . I can't move, I can't think, I can't call my girlfriend!" Then I was in total bliss. All thinking was nonexistent. One color after the other was showering my being with rays of indescribable love and light! Amazing, indescribable bliss! After the last color it turned white, again with a special new aspect of this love of each color. Then I saw three people and the ship looked like a little cute recording studio/office. They did not look at me or show any reaction. Then I can't remember how I went to my bed. I woke up in the morning, the memory of this nighttime event very strong in my head, jumping out of my bed, realizing the curtains are open, realizing after the last moment of what I could remember—seeing the three people—I must have landed back in my bed again. I went downstairs to find Sascha and I told her everything. She said that she was also waking up in the middle of the night, watching "flying lights in the night sky" but not getting out of bed. She pointed to my tummy and said, "They brought you Cosma!" I said, "What a beautiful name!"

I went to Dr. Parker in the Santa Monica area, and he was guiding me through my pregnancy. I went to yoga and ate healthy food. Then on May 16 we went to an open-air reggae festival in LA and I felt my tummy falling down. It was a new pressure that I felt. I ate a grilled fish and went home to sleep. In the very early morning hours I went to pee and when I realized that my water has broken, I liked the smell, because it smelled like the ocean and my boyfriend! We called Dr. Parker. He told me to wait for the "waves" to recur every five minutes or less and if I want, come on over to the hospital any time. So we prepared. I took it easy, enjoying every single wave. I got so high! Sooo happy, looking forward to each new wave. Now we were already in the hospital and I went through labor all day. I had difficulty standing the strong waves, squeezing my girlfriend's hand. (At my second birth I cuddled with my boyfriend and was open in less than one hour, ready to push, but then the pushing part took eight hours! That was with my second child, Otis, nine years later!) So, after all day laboring at Santa Monica Hospital, I finally, around 7:30 P.M., felt the urge to press. I pressed once. I pressed twice. At the third press the baby landed at a very painful spot, and I started to get hysterical. Dr. Parker told me to keep breathing normal. I thought "What? Normal? Is he crazy?!" Now I understand. The next wave came. I pushed. Dr. Parker made a nice cut, didn't hurt at all. I think he gave me a needle of pain-number before. And finally my sweet daughter was born! I said, "Is it black or white?" They yelled, "It's a girl! It's a girl!" They gave her to me. I was in heaven also spiritually! I saw her as a little baby Buddha. I was totally happy! By the way, Cosma was born on May 17 at 8:14 P.M., and my second child, Otis, was born on August 3 at 8:14 A.M.!

When I was pregnant with Otis, I had many great and special dreams during our pregnancy, and I have gotten instant answers to personal and spiritual questions in my naptime dreams. I felt very close, especially close to Jesus and Babaji during that time. Also, Otis's birth was very dangerous. Somehow he was a much bigger baby than Cosma, and during labor, my two midwives, who were at my home, hoping and planning on a home birth, started to look scared after I tried in vain to push for two hours. We hurried up to the hospital, which was horrible. The midwife was only allowed to perform her work when she brought me to a faraway hospital in the urban outskirts of Paris, even though there was a hospital just around the corner from where we were living. So I had to push all through the ride along the freeway, and with the help of three more midwives, I finally gave birth to Otis in the morning. I made a pledge with God that time, where I asked Him or Her for a boon, of not having to come back to planet Earth anymore, and also for my son and daughter, that he and she and I might attain Buddhahood after this life.

Kimberly: Did you breastfeed?

Nina: Breastfeeding was great. I had no problems. I did massage my breasts and the nipples during pregnancy also. I put Ringelblumen-salbe on and massaged [them]. Cosma was breastfed until she was one year old. One morning she simply said, "No!" in the sweetest baby voice. "No" was her first word!

Otis was breastfed only for four months. He wanted a bottle very early. When both children were born I had a lot of time for them and me. With Cosma, we went to the Bahamas the first three months, then to New York, where we recorded *NunSexMonkRock,* but Cosma got the first cough of her life. It was so cold in New York, so I went to Jamaica with her, just the two of us.

Kimberly: What kind of help and support did you have from family and friends?

Nina: Cosma's dad, Ferdinand, was visiting us the day she was born at the hospital, but Cosma has really never seen him or spent any time with him. Cosma's father was addicted to drugs—heroin—and died when Cosma was 10 years old. Otis's father, Frank, was there at the birth, and when we broke up when Otis was two, we remained good friends. Otis spends all his holidays with his dad.

With both children, I had the help of wonderful girlfriends and nannies, who were always traveling with us—when we had to go on tour, for example.

Kimberly: How did you balance work and motherhood? You did incredible work when Cosma was a baby. How did you do it?

Nina: The children were always with me, and I did not tour as extensively as other rock artists. I preferred the special status of being an underground gem. We lived in Spain for four years on the beautiful island of Ibiza; in Paris three years; in LA first for five years, then in the '90s again for three years. Now we live in Berlin. Cosma is 21 years old; she is a very popular actress here in Germany, and she also organizes big and beautiful open-air festivals, where she invites me and my band to do the warm-up. Otis goes to school here in Berlin and right now he is on holiday with his dad.

Kimberly: What's the coolest thing about being a mother?

Nina: These two indescribably wonderful children are the *joy* and the *love* of my life! [Motherhood has changed me] totally! They are my gurus! My life! They made me even more aware of the deep respect and love for God and His Creation, us!

Kimberly: How do you teach them about spirituality?

Nina: Well, my children are still traveling with me sometimes, for example to my friends' ashram in India. I made a film about it, *Om Gottes Willen/Om Namah Shivay*. And they have reached a warm and spiritual understanding that all religions and all people are equal and to follow the religion of your heart, and that service to other people, humanitarian causes, are the true religion. To be human and help each other.

Kimberly: Do you have any advice for mothers of teenagers?

Nina: First of all, I have to remind myself of [my own teenage years]. I was sometimes repelled, sometimes in need of my mother. Bearing all this in mind, I tried to cool down a lot of moments and situations between my daughter during puberty and me. Little brother Otis was there, and so I realized that at age 13, she wanted to be free to decide where to live. And it was a really nice boarding school, nearby Hamburg, where many of her schoolmates from Ibiza went to now, and also where her grandmother lives. She had a steady boyfriend (just like I did) at an early age. She was then allowed to move in together with him at my mother's house. I missed her terribly, and I'm sure that she missed me and Otis also, but we visited each other a lot and also spend holidays together in Ibiza, where we lived for four years before Otis was born. We have a home there. She still spends as much of her time as possible with us. She also started working as an actress very early. Advice for moms with teenagers? I have none except: Trust in God and His ways, give your child as much of your time, your love, your understanding, et cetera, as possible!

News Flash

Universe Running Away with Itself

There's new evidence from more than a dozen exploding stars in the most distant reaches of space that a mysterious kind of antigravity energy is speeding the expansion of the universe. Astronomers and other scientists are amazed. It seems that the universe is defying Einstein's predictions, as well as common sense, and is running away with itself. Its outer edges could continue running forever, and at ever-increasing speeds.

When *Hip Mama* editor's daughter heard about this, she got a mischievous little gleam in her eye. "Is it gonna blow?"

"Naw," she was assured.

She seemed a little disappointed.

A Woman Named Mary

Nanci Olesen

Every woman who has ever given birth loves to tell her story. She loves to tell it in excruciating detail. She'll tell it to anyone who will listen.

One ravenous night some 2,000 years ago, a woman named Mary brought a baby into the world and laid him in swaddling clothes in the manger. It's the ultimate birth story, I guess.

Now that I've birthed a few children myself, I can't help but think of the whole story in a new light. Now that I know the howl of the moment of birth, the awesome pain and the unrecognizable joy, the unbelievable relief of having completed a task that took my body over completely and brought me to the end of the earth and back, I look at those nativity scenes quite differently. She always looks serene, Mary. She sometimes looks a bit possessed. I think I understand.

I look at Mary's face whenever I see her—people's front lawns, store windows, Christmas cards. There she is and there's that expression. Radiant.

I imagine that we are seeing her several hours after the big event.

I think of that time, the first hours after the birth of a baby. Someone has to help you sit up; maybe you've gone so far as to brush your hair. Your forehead has been washed with a warm cloth. You've had a drink of water. Your still-shaking hands reach for the baby, the babe who has been born, of all things. You gaze in wonderment at the face and hands of that glorious child. The face of a stranger, the face of someone you've known all your life. Every minute detail of a human being. You have no idea what the next 33 years are going to hold for this little person . . . or for you as the mother of this person. Who is this? The wave of love and joy and amazement will perhaps never be stronger than at this moment.

And that's how you see Mary, over and over, in every artist's rendering . . . an hour or so after . . . and she kneels before this baby, with her arms open. Radiant joy. Radiant hope. Radiant love.

Letters to the Editor

Thank You for Canceling My Subscription

Thanks so much for taking the time to read this message. Since subscribing to your magazine, I have accepted Jesus Christ into my life and have begun to study the Bible as the Word of God. I am no longer interested in the themes and ideas expressed in your articles. I also must comment on the recent article denouncing Christian parenting and the Promise Keepers. Although I have some conflicts with the Promise Keepers regarding religious separation, I must comment on the idea of submission in marriage and family that feminists seem to rally against. If you read Ephesians, Chapter 5, you will have a full understanding that as wives, we are to submit just as husbands are to honor and love their wives and treat them with the same love and reverence with which Jesus treats the church. It seems ironic to me that the same people who demand tolerance are the people who are least willing to give it. It is my hope and prayer for all of you that you embrace Jesus Christ as your savior. It is an awfully long eternity.

Thank you for canceling my subscription.

Paula Bento

Vermont

Go Mama!

Dear Hip Mama,

Thanks for being "all" the women in me! As I read over your latest issue I call my best girl, who is going through a messy divorce, and preach, "Hip Mama is for you! I can't tell you what you're missing!"

She replies with the usual, "Are you still subscribing to all those mothering magazines?"

No, Hip Mama is different. It helps me to grasp all the women/mamas I am on/in various days, times, and years of my life. There are times when I feel I am a mother of twins, a wife, and a working member of society. There are days when I want the house clean, dinner on the table, and the kids in tow; and there are weeks when the laundry never gets done, takeout is our only fare, and the kids are running around naked all day. Days when all I want to do is smoke and hang out with a friend; and times when my work is the last thing on my mind.

I am the one who asks, "Is it too early for a beer?"

Hip Mama has helped me to realize that there are other women out there like me, those not-so-perfect mamas, those "real" mamas.

I am a woman with many friends—divorced, single, married, and gay. Some are on welfare and some are high on the hog. Your mag can relate to us all.

My best girl calls and asks if my sex life is passionate, wild, and wonderful. "Are the kids great? And do you love your life?" I reply, "There are days when it's yes, and days when it is not."

Keep up the inspiring, thought-provoking work.

Maternally Yours,

Stephanie Shamsuddin

Birmingham, Alabama

Lineage

Sunday	Monday	Tuesday	Wednesday
3 Kid wants to find Jesus. Find liberal church instead.	**4** Get $120 in food stamps! Buy spaghetti & pies.	**5** Cancel therapy. Neglect family. See Resident Bush on TV. Cry for three hours.	**6** Sister comes to visit with kid & Italian boyfriend. Lose boyfriend in forest.
10 Priest sez: The time to pray for peace is over. Start praying for miracles.	**11** Strange astrological convergence results in total nervous breakdown.	**12** Cancel therapy. Watch CNN & fall into deeper depression. Go to grotto to pray.	**13** Run into a scary part of my brain. Try & do yoga to get out of it. Strain neck.
17 Sleep in. Miss church. Kid gets kitten that cries like a newborn human.	**18** Spend all day cleaning up kitten shit.	**19** Cancel therapy. See *Bowling for Columbine.* Plan move to Canada.	**20** Get stuck in freak blizzard on the way to Canada.
24 Notice FBI has searched house while we were at church.	**25** Dream that I get six years in prison for decorating house à la Martha Stewart.	**26** Make yummy tamale pie on dwindling food stamp budget.	**27** Cancel therapy. Start chanting "I am a money magnet" mantra.

Thursday	Friday	Saturday
	1 What? No child support check? Again? Attempt to overthrow government.	**2** Take kid to football game, then to Italian lesson. Start working on anthology.
7 Search party finds boyfriend. He sez: "I only stopped to make a pee."	**8** Start hoarding water for apocalypse. Get back to work on anthology.	**9** Get confused—who's winning football game? Clap at inappropriate moments.
14 Run away from home to follow Rolling Thunder Democracy Tour.	**15** Protest at state capitol. Get ticketed for "stopping illegally."	**16** Get in fight with hot-dog-headed football fan at kid's game.
21 Stay in cheap motel in Nowheresville. Wonder if this is the apocalypse.	**22** Fly to Miami to meet new in-laws. Kid gets stung by jellyfish.	**23** Fly home on SWA via Orlando, Nashville, Oakland, Reno. Shouldda hitchhiked.
28 Trade in computer for laptop so we'll be able to flee country quicker.	**29** Two espresso shots & a jug of wine: up all night finishing anthology.	**30** Turn in anthology! Kid graduates from 8th grade. Bawl at ceremony.

yo mama's daybook

Mama Said: The Best and Worst Advice We Ever Got from Our Mothers

Inga, 30

The best advice I didn't take: "Don't marry that man."
Worst: My dad told me that I'd better learn how to cook or no man would ever want to marry me.

Tibor, 30

Worst: "Make something of yourself; join the Hungarian Communist Youth Alliance."

Julie, 25

Best: When I got pregnant when I was 17, she said, "Do you want to get an abortion?" I said, "No." She said, "Are you ready to be a mother?" I said, "I don't know." So she said, "Well, you better get ready."

James, 31

Best: When I separated from my wife, she said, "Either get back together or file for divorce. Don't live in limbo."

Worst: "Don't count your chickens before they hatch." Okay, we lived in Arkansas.

Ariel, 25
Best: "Don't lose track of who's crazy and who's not."
Worst: "If you put it on a credit card, it's free."

More than Plastic Sushi

Susan Ito

"What are you, anyway?"

I've had to confront this question hundreds of times during my childhood and adult years, and it's one that's not unfamiliar to most biracial people. We're mysterious. Curious. Different. Genetically, I am half Japanese American. Culturally, I'm 100 percent. Although I was conceived by a Japanese mother and a white father (ethnicity unknown), I was adopted as an infant by two Nisei or second-generation Japanese American parents. I ate teriyaki hot dogs, learned to count *ichi, ni, san* with my grandmother, and was called home at dinnertime by the deep boom of a ceremonial gong. Except for the times that I looked into a mirror or glanced at a family photograph, I never felt like half.

My daughter Mollie, who was born with a headful of black hair and crinkly brown eyes, is gene-wise only a quarter Asian. Her dad is Irish-Texan and New Orleans–French. It's unlikely that she'll be asked The Question as much as I was. It'll be easy for her to "pass." And I mourn her passing.

My grandmother, who spoke no more than a hundred words of

English, died when Mollie was a year old, so my daughter won't be immersed in Japanese like I was. My parents spoke Japanese when my grandmother was around, so I used the two languages interchangeably. But now that she's gone, all Mollie hears is English and Spanish from our Nicaraguan housemates. She's more likely to use the word *arroz* for rice than *gohan*. And that makes me sad.

I try to compensate in small, ridiculous ways. Through a mail-order catalog I was able to order plastic sushi and rice balls for her pretend dinner parties. The family in her dollhouse all have little black rice-bowl haircuts, and tiny black almond-shaped eyes. But they're lost in the toy box, hardly noticeable when they're tossed in a jumble with Bert and Ernie, My Little Pony, and the stuffed armadillo.

I admit that I could take it further, if it really mattered that much. I could commute 45 minutes each morning and afternoon and enroll her in a Japanese preschool. I could seek out Japanese-speaking babysitters and other people to talk with my children. But I don't. Am I lazy? No. But I'm shy—I worry that somehow I'm not "Japanese enough." People might look at me funny and think, "What is she doing here?" When I was younger, my parents were the ambassadors who gained me passage into the larger Japanese community. Without them, I'm afraid my 50 percent isn't enough to carry my entire family. In just one generation, the "Japaneseness" in our family has nearly evaporated.

I recently saw a video on biracial people where the narrator commented about always being shocked when she looked in the mirror. Raised by her East Indian mother and grandmother for nearly her entire life, she saw them as her most significant role models. Her absent father's Danish genes, resulting in a light complexion, was not what she expected to see. I can relate to this. I am always so much less Asian-looking on the outside than how I feel on the inside.

Emma, my second daughter, has blue-gray eyes and hair the color of a gingerbread cookie. The Asian genes in her are no more than a sprinkling. People do a double take when they see her Nisei grandparents pushing her in the stroller. I've given her my grandmother's name, Asano, as a middle name. Perhaps as my daughters grow up they'll wonder about this part of themselves (is it half or is it a quarter of who they are?). It's more than plastic sushi or knowing how to fold an origami crane, or even the exuberance of the *taiko* drumming classes I've planned for Mollie. It's a feeling of being 100 percent themselves, all their perfect parts combined.

News Flash

People Came from Nowhere

Survival of the fittest? Darwin is dead. And his legacy may or may not survive.

Seventy years after John Scopes was found guilty of teaching evolution in Dayton, Tennessee, the legislature there began considering letting school boards dismiss teachers who presented evolution as fact rather than theory.

Meanwhile, a Georgia district okayed the teaching of creationism, and Alabama approved a disclaimer to be inserted in biology books calling evolution "only a controversial theory."

The result? Teaching where humans came from has become so politicized that many teachers are reportedly skipping over the entire issue to avoid risking confrontations with parents, and instead adopting something of a don't-ask, don't-tell policy about the origin of the species.

CREATIONIST'S "DON'T ASK - DON'T TELL" POLICY

"Are you now, or have you ever been, genetically related to the human race?"   D. LEE

Hip Mama Asks: What's Your Lineage?

Lineage. Blood and genes. Traditions of caring. Predecessors, living and dead. Footsteps to walk in and footsteps to walk clear of. Does ancestry matter? *Hip Mama* asked 13 writers to share their lines.

My Lineage Drives a Pea-Green Pinto

My lineage drives a pea-green Pinto and smells like Tab when she burps, which is often. My lineage picks me up on Wednesdays after school when she remembers, which is not often. My lineage tells me what an asshole my father is while she drives me to the house she shares with a man named Stewart and a boat that says, "Kiss my Bass." I spend the day weeding the garden with my lineage, until she takes me back to my father. In the car, as she sits beside me and gives off soda burps, she says, "I will never leave you again."

Within a year, my lineage moves to Delaware, gets married, has a daughter, and becomes someone else's lineage.

—Shanna Germain

Perpetual Disconnect

On a good day I come from a long line of colorful folk: Creek and Seminole, African, African American, Puerto Rican, Dominican, Irish, and whatever else is mixed in there. We have a history of education and being seekers in the world. On a bad day, I come from a long line of alcoholics, keepers of secrets, and disconnected people.

I often wonder what will happen to my kids. Will they long for connection to rich histories and partner with people who have such families and become immersed? Or might they go on to connect with people and things, as I have, that perpetuate the disconnect?

—Inga Aaron

Transplanted

Word has it I'm French-Irish on one side and Scottish on the other, descended from the dour portrait of a scrawny old gent that hangs above my father's desk—hard to believe this Puritanical-looking fellow was kicked out of Edinburgh University for partying too hard and moved to America where springtime revealed that he had impregnated his landlord's daughter—a farmer's daughter, no less. On the maternal side, my grandfather's late-onset mania for genealogy has turned up lots of short-lived English people with names like Experience, Consider, and Thankful Bullock. We wanted to name Inky "Mehitabel," after an obscure relative footnoted on one of the unwieldy printouts, but Grampy was the only family member who approved. My father's mother spent the last 15 years of her life in Tucson, Arizona, immersing herself, aesthetically anyway, in American Indian artwork, jewelry, and lore. She insisted that I, with my long dark braids and easily tanned skin, had Cherokee (princess!) blood, but my father, in Indiana, remained skeptical.

I think the ethnic legacy I'll pass on is Hoosier transplanted to New York City.

—Ayun Halliday

My Mom . . .
She Takes care of me.
She Takes me To places
and feeds me.
She is Chinese and
American. She is sTill
learning English.
She someTimes
geTs mad aT me, buT I
sTill love her.
—Eric, age eighT

Creator of the Alphabet

In my culture, spirit and souls are constantly being revived through the death, birth, and marriage of family members. Many people in my family believe that my son is the reincarnated soul of my grandfather. Also, my mom and aunts believe that I have the spirit of my grandmother because she was feisty, strong, and visionary. Koreans put a lot of stock into family ancestry and lineage. Your name not only identifies you, but is the foundation for who you can become and an indication of who your ancestors were. I am a direct descendant of King Sejong, who created the Korean alphabet. My family believes that our family's love of words and communication developed centuries ago. You think about your name and upholding its value and continuing its worth. I have come to believe that lineage is just like everything else in life: You take what is useful from the past to apply to your future, and discard the rest. I claim my lineage of strong women from the Kim side and my love of words from the Lee side, and I know that my grandmother's determination carries me through the most difficult of times—through my dreams and intuition.

—Soo Young Lee

My Dog Knows More

When I think of lineage, it makes me realize that my dog had more information on his bloodline than I do. I was adopted, and most of my "lineage" is pretty fuzzy. I know I'm half Japanese and half . . . it's anybody's guess. Sometimes this makes me feel really unsubstantial, and ungrounded. My parents' parents, I'm told, were stowaways on a boat from Japan and aren't registered at Ellis Island or anywhere else. We're a bunch of undocumented, unpapered, unofficial illegals. My adoptive parents never knew their own grandparents' names, so our known lineage is pretty short. I try to tell myself that papers aren't the same as identity, but still, it would be nice to be publicly recorded somewhere.

—Susan Ito

Like My Mother Before Me

The Merriam-Webster's dictionary tells me that "lineage" is a bloodline, a pedigree, filiation, origin, ancestry, and a derivation. It can also mean the rate of payment for the number of lines in a piece of written work. I am a woman and a mother like my mother before me, and my grandmother before her. We are Canadian, which means I'm a mutt. And I've never been paid for anything I've written.

—Lindsey Campbell-Rock

Stone Churches

Lineage: great aunts I never knew, distant cousins I never saw, cold air, stone churches. My father's temper, my mother's tantrums. Constant grief enclosed in a great airy blanket of dumb sunlight.

—M. F. McAuliffe

The New World

A trio of Spanish men: two sons and their father. They came to the new world, South America, back in the day, to see if it was something they would like to exploit. One of the boys decided to make a go of it. From his decision comes my paternal line. Through the years, his descendants have included adventurers, priests, politicians, and the great great great great grandmother who had eight children by the slave who killed her husband. This clan is rich in anecdotes and stories that survive, somehow, through the butchering of their telling by each generation. Each generation is prolific, and everyone sticks around close to home. My maternal side is silent, silent for the guilt-ridden pleasure of having secrets. Very few stories circulate. The past is not talked about. A few stay close to home, and have many children. But most, myself included, fly the coop. Far. And become estranged from the others.

—Maria Fabulosa

The Legacy Ends Here

One would be hard-pressed to find a woman in either of my biological lines who was not victimized by a violent partner. I'm not sure how far back it goes, but I don't imagine that my mother seeing her own mother ridiculed for "falling down the stairs" and breaking her ribs by the man who pushed her did anything to empower her when she was in her first or second or third abusive relationship. In my branch of the family tree, the legacy ends here, and I fervently wish the same for my cousins, whose mothers all married abusive men who were not unlike their fathers.

—Dorie Lanni

Cake Batter with a Straw

What is lineage? No, really—is that like heritage? I come from a long line of guilt-ridden heavy eaters. By that I don't just mean we're guilty over eating heavily. And we're not just heavy eaters as in we weigh too much. I mean we feel guilty about everything and we discuss it while eating heavy foods. Whenever I go back to Jersey (AKA "land of my people") I can expect food groups that include "cake batter with a straw" counting as a smoothie and cheese hoagies to cleanse the palate between breakfast and dinner.

Seriously, when you ask about lineage, I think of family, and when I think about family, since I come from a family that never kept too much track of our ancestors (we're maybe from Scotland or maybe Ireland with a little Kraut thrown in), I think of my immediate relatives. And even that I narrow down to just a few sisters. Okay, four sisters. I have seven but I only see four of them with any regularity.

—Spike Gillespie

Romantic and Obscure

I feel very attached to the fact that I'm Polish. I guess the Polish side of my family is less diluted, so it seems like I'm more that; or I have my birth father's nature and he is, like, 100 percent Polish. The rest of me is Irish, and it's very embarrassing to be Irish where I come from—Boston. Too often Irish stands for White Power over there, so early on I began to disown it. I'm also a tad English—blah, a tad French—very vague, and the teeniest smidgen of Native American—yeah, right, all white people like to think they've got the teeniest smidgen of Native American in them. I mean, I think I really do, but still, it's even more embarrassing than the Irish thing, but for different reasons . . . Polish seems sort of romantic and obscure. I like it. I keep trying to find my Polish relations online but I can't. If anyone knows any Swankowskis in Poland, they're my people and I'd like to meet them.

Otherwise, I feel like I'm part of a disenfranchised queer writing lineage that includes Eileen Myles and Violette Leduc, or at least I'd like to think I am.

—Michelle Tea

My Mom

My mom is like an unfinished drawing
missing loTs of pieces.
She's noT perfecT buT she does her besT and
she gives iT her all, even When she falls
she geTs back up and Tries again.
She's like a machine. She Turns on
all day and aT nighT she recharges
her baTTeries. She sTands up for me from
man or beasT. I love her and all buT
someTimes she geTs mad aT me. BuT
When she goes iT will be a loss. Because
we all love her and she would be hard
To leT go. I love my mom, she is good
To me and I am going To enjoy my mom

and all her love
because she is my best friend
To The end
and I love her.
—Jonathan Escobar, age nine

How to Make Ariel's Childhood Thanksgiving Dinner

Eve DeBona

Menu
Roast Turkey with Cornbread Stuffing and Pan Gravy
Cranberry-Orange Relish
Broccoli al Dente
Candied Yams
Wine
Sparkling Cider for the kids
Pumpkin Chiffon Pie
Coffee and Tea

Take five days to prepare this feast. Do a little each day and get lots of help. Ask guests to bring hors d'oeuvres, side dishes, dinner rolls, the wines and sparkling ciders, and another dessert if there are to be more than 10 people.

Suggested Game Plan:

Sunday: Go to market; order turkey.

Monday: Make cranberry-orange relish. Make cornbread for stuffing.

Tuesday: Make pumpkin chiffon pie.

Wednesday: Pick up turkey and buy broccoli. Prepare broccoli for cooking. Make turkey stock. Make candied yams. Prepare stuffing tonight and/or in morning.

Thursday: Prepare or finish preparing stuffing. Prepare and roast turkey. Bake the candied yams. Prepare broccoli. Make gravy.

MONDAY:

Cranberry-Orange Relish

$1/2$ cup water

$1/2$ cup fresh-squeezed orange juice

1 cup granulated sugar

1 lb. whole fresh cranberries

2 tablespoons orange zest (or grated orange rind)

In a 3- to 4-quart saucepan, stir water, orange juice, and sugar together until sugar is thoroughly dissolved. Add cranberries, bring to a boil, and cook for 3 to 5 minutes, stirring occasionally, until skins of berries begin to pop and berries are tender but not mushy. *Do not overcook them.*

Remove pan from heat and stir in orange rind. Transfer mixture to a serving bowl, let cool, then cover and refrigerate. Makes 1 quart.

Cornbread

(This cornbread is specifically for stuffing; otherwise you need to add $^1/_3$ cup sugar.)
Have all ingredients at room temperature.
1 $^1/_2$ cups yellow cornmeal
1 cup all-purpose flour
1 teaspoon salt
1 tablespoon baking powder
2 eggs
1 cube melted and cooled butter (never use margarine or other substitute)
1 $^1/_2$ cups milk
Preheat oven to 400° F. Sift the cornmeal, flour, salt, and baking powder into a mixing bowl. Beat eggs lightly, add melted butter, and stir in milk. Pour these liquids into the bowl of dry ingredients and beat together for about a minute or until smooth. Do not overbeat. Lightly butter a 9" x 5" x 3" loaf pan or 8" x 12" shallow baking pan and pour in batter. Bake in center of oven about 30 minutes or until bread comes slightly away from edge of pan and is golden brown. When cooled to room temperature, wrap and refrigerate until time to make stuffing.

TUESDAY:

Gammie Garrett's Pumpkin Chiffon Pie*

Crumb Crust
1 $^1/_2$ cups (4 $^1/_2$ oz.) gingersnap crumbs
2 tablespoons sugar
pinch of salt

$1/2$ cup (4 oz.) unsalted butter, melted

Preheat oven to 325° F. Gingersnaps are crisp, not cakey, and must be fresh. Crush them with a rolling pin, or, better yet, make the crumbs in a food processor. Combine crumbs, sugar, and salt in mixing bowl and stir together. Add melted butter and stir until well blended. Press and pat mixture over bottom and sides of 9" pie pan. Don't make sides too thick. Bake crust 8 minutes and cool completely before filling.

Filling

3 fresh organic eggs, separated

1 cup sugar

1 $1/4$ cups fresh baked and puréed pumpkin, or canned pumpkin

$1/2$ cup milk

$1/2$ teaspoon each salt, nutmeg, cinnamon, and ginger

$1/4$ cup cold water

1 envelope unflavored gelatin

$1/2$ pint whipping cream

To slightly beaten egg yolks add $1/2$ cup of the sugar, the pumpkin, milk, salt, and spices. Cook in top of double boiler until thick, stirring constantly; don't let it get lumpy. Pour the cold water into a small bowl and sprinkle gelatin on top. Let stand 5 minutes. Add this to hot pumpkin mixture. Mix thoroughly, then cool. When it begins to thicken add remaining sugar and fold in stiffly beaten egg whites. Pour into crust and refrigerate.

Whip the cream. (Do not sweeten the cream; the pie is very sweet.) Cover tightly and refrigerate.

Take pie out of refrigerator 15 minutes before serving so crust doesn't stick to pan. Serve with the whipped cream.

*If you are concerned about the fact that the Pumpkin Chiffon Pie contains uncooked egg whites, use pasteurized eggs or try this recipe instead:

Pumpkin Pie

Unless you make a great pie crust, just buy a prepared one (NOT whole wheat), 8" to 9 $^1/_2$" inches in diameter. Thaw it if it has been frozen, but don't let it get warm; you want it chilly. With a table fork prick the bottom and sides—including where they meet—at $^1/_2$-inch intervals. Flatten a 11" square of aluminum foil inside the shell, pressing it flush against corners, sides, and over rim. Prick foil bottom in about a dozen places with fork. Chill shell an hour or more.

Adjust oven racks to lowest and middle positions, and heat oven to 375° F. (Start preparing filling when you put shell in oven, as you want both shell and filling hot when you assemble the pie.) Partially bake pie shell on middle rack for 15 minutes, pressing down on foil with mitt-protected hand to flatten any puffs. Remove foil and bake shell about 8 to 10 minutes longer or until interior just begins to color.

Filling
2 cups (16 oz.) plain canned pumpkin purée
1 cup packed dark brown sugar
2 teaspoons ground ginger
2 teaspoons ground cinnamon
1 teaspoon fresh grated nutmeg
$^1/_2$ teaspoon ground cloves
$^1/_2$ teaspoon salt
Process all ingredients in a food processor (with a steel blade), put through a food mill, or force through a fine sieve with the back of a wooden spoon.

Process for 1 minute. Transfer mixture to a 3-quart heavy-bottomed saucepan; bring it to a sputtering simmer over medium-high heat. Cook, stirring constantly, until thick and shiny, about 5 minutes. As soon as pie shell comes out of oven, increase oven temperature to 400° F.

Now you need:
2/3 cup heavy cream
2/3 cup milk
4 large eggs
Whisk cream and milk into pumpkin and bring to barely a simmer. Process eggs in food processor until whites and yolks are mixed, about 5 seconds. With motor running, slowly pour about half of hot pumpkin mixture through feed tube. Stop machine and scrape in remaining pumpkin. Process 30 seconds longer.

Immediately pour warm filling into hot pie shell. (Ladle any excess filling into pie after pie has baked for 5 minutes or so, when filling has settled.) Bake pie on lower rack about 25 minutes, until filling is puffed, dry-looking, and lightly cracked around edges, and center wiggles like gelatin when pie is gently shaken. Residual heat will finish the cooking outside the oven. Cool on a wire rack for at least 1 hour.

Brandied Whipped Cream Topping (for adults):
1 1/3 cups heavy cream, cold
2 tablespoons sugar
1 tablespoon brandy
When ready to serve pie, beat cream and sugar with an electric mixer at medium speed to soft peaks; add brandy. Beat to stiff peaks. Ac-

company each wedge of pie with a dollop of this, but serve the children's pie plain.

WEDNESDAY:

Stock for Gravy

Get giblets (minus liver, which you'll use in stuffing) and neck out of turkey (probably in a little bag in body cavity). Put these in a saucepan with a little onion, carrot, celery, salt, pepper, and 4 cups water. Simmer about an hour. Strain and refrigerate. Now you have stock to use for gravy. Chop giblets finely and save, refrigerated, for gravy also. Give turkey neck to the cat.

Ariel's Dad's Candied Yams

12 medium-sized yams
Salt and paprika
1 ½ cups brown sugar
1 teaspoon lemon zest (or grated lemon rind)
3 tablespoons lemon juice or ¼ teaspoon grated fresh ginger (peeled)
4 tablespoons butter
Preheat oven to 375° F. To cook yams in their jackets, drop them into boiling water to cover and cook in a covered pot about 25 minutes or until tender. Cool and then peel. Cut lengthwise in ½-inch slices or mash them. Set aside a bit for the baby. Put the rest in a shallow buttered baking dish. Season with salt and paprika. Sprinkle with the brown sugar, lemon zest, and lemon juice or ginger. Dot with butter. Bake uncovered

about 20 minutes, or cover and refrigerate until time to bake, then bring to room temperature before putting in oven.

Cornbread Stuffing

10 tablespoons butter

1 ½ cups finely chopped onion

1 pound Italian sausage meat

the turkey liver (it's probably in the turkey cavity, along with rest of giblets and neck)

6 cups of the cornbread, coarsely crumbled (give the rest to the chickens)

½ teaspoon salt

freshly ground black pepper

2 teaspoons thyme

¼ cup finely chopped fresh parsley

¼ cup Madeira or sherry

¼ cup heavy cream

Melt 8 tablespoons of the butter in a heavy skillet, add chopped onions and cook over moderate heat 6 to 8 minutes or until they color lightly. Scrape into large mixing bowl. Squeeze sausage meat out of casing and put in same skillet, set over medium heat. Break up meat as it cooks. When meat is lightly browned, transfer to a sieve set over a small bowl and let fat drain through. Meanwhile in same pan melt remaining 2 tablespoons butter; when foam subsides add turkey liver. Brown it over high heat 2 to 3 minutes, then chop it coarsely and combine it with onions in bowl. Add drained sausage meat, cornbread crumbs, salt, a few grindings black pepper, thyme, and parsley. *If preparing this the night before, stop here, cover and refrigerate. Take out of fridge first thing in the morning.* Gently stir together with large spoon, then moisten stuffing with the Madeira or sherry, and cream. Taste for seasoning.

Wait to stuff the bird until just before roasting, and loosely fill only ¾ full (because it will expand).

THURSDAY:

Roast Stuffed Turkey

Try to get an organic bird, or at least one that has not been fed hormones and antibiotics.

Have a 10- to 16-pound turkey at about 70° F before roasting. Allow 20 to 25 minutes per pound roasting time.

Preheat oven to 450° F. Melt a cube of butter. Wash bird under cold running water, rinsing out cavities, and dry it inside and out. (Take care not to puncture or tear skin.) Never salt it. Stuff crop and cavity with the cornbread stuffing, and sew those openings shut or use safety pins to close them. Tie ends of legs together so they will stay close to the body, and bind wings close to body too, unless bird fits very snugly into roasting pan. Set stuffed and trussed bird on oiled rack in roasting pan, breast side up. With a pastry brush, brush outside of bird with a few tablespoons of the melted butter. Place turkey uncovered in oven and immediately reduce heat to 350° F. Continue brushing with melted butter every 20 minutes while bird cooks, until you can start basting with pan drippings every 20 minutes, using the brush or preferably a bulb baster. If bird is getting too brown before it's done, cover roasting pan with lid (not with foil—you don't want to use aluminum foil in the oven). Cook to an internal temperature of 190° F. If you don't have a meat thermometer, prick the skin of the thigh to see if the juice runs clear, and jiggle the drumsticks to see if hip joints are loose. When you are sure it's done, let it sit on a warm platter while you make gravy.

Pan Gravy

Skim fat from pan juices into small bowl. Pour defatted pan juices into another bowl, scraping bottom of pan with wooden spoon to get all stuck bits. Pour 3 tablespoons of the fat into small skillet. Add 3 tablespoons flour and stir over low heat until flour is absorbed and slightly toasted; you don't want the taste of raw flour. Add 2 cups of liquid—the degreased pan juices and the stock you made yesterday. Bring to a boil and simmer, stirring constantly with a wire whisk until gravy is thick and smooth. Don't let it get lumpy. If it gets too thick add more stock, or add milk or cream or beer or water. Season with salt and pepper and the giblets you chopped. Pour into a warm sauceboat or pitcher and serve.

Broccoli al Dente

Very green and firm heads of broccoli
Salt
Butter
Lemon juice
Remove leaves and cut off tough lower stalks. Give leaves to the rabbit. (Even he won't eat tough stalks.) Separate heads into florets of about equal size so they cook evenly. Use only about first 3 inches of stem, and even so peel tough outer skin off. Wash under cold running water, or if buggy soak 15 minutes in salted water or vinegar water. *Do this much the day before; cover and refrigerate until ready to cook.*
    Cook broccoli in lots of simmering, salted water for no more than

5 minutes. A bit of sugar in the water will help broccoli stay greener. (Leave a bit of broccoli in pot and cook until soft for the baby.) Drain it and sprinkle it with a little salt. Put in a warm serving bowl and serve with a little melted butter and lemon juice.

Grandma Is Old and Has White Hair

Geraldo Valério

Grandma lives alone. Her house is blue and has gray wood windows. Her house is in the middle of a garden. There is a lawn with a strange kind of plant covering the ground. This plant has small round leaves and sometimes little yellow flowers bloom. There are also amaryllis, begonias, white roses, and white camellias.

In the backyard there is an orange tree. The orange tree is so tall that we cannot reach the fruit. We have to grab them with a hook. They are big oranges and they come in many shades between green and orange. The orange ones are the most flavorful. They are warm and full of juice. An orange like that, you don't eat it—you drink it. You suck, you suck, and the orange slowly goes inside of you.

Grandma is able to peel an orange, cutting its skin in a long and continuous strip. Grandma will peel as many oranges as we want. So many oranges fill the air with a sweet and acidic smell.

Grandma is old and has white hair. Her head is all white. She sometimes passes her hand through her hair, gently pulling the ones that are falling out. She grabs them and keeps them in her hands.

Grandma is always wearing a coat. It is never hot enough for her to take it off. She says it is because of a fever that she had. Scarlet fever.

During her illness, she says she was burning for days and it was a miracle that she survived. She tells me that because of this fever she lost all the hair on her body. She was left only with the hair on her head and that since the scarlet fever she has always been cold.

"This coldness comes from inside." She points to her chest.

Grandma looks down at her dress and starts pulling one hair here and another there. Then, softly, almost not wanting to be heard, she says that she believes that dead people can come back. She says that one night, she came to the kitchen and there was a woman dressed in white sitting on the wood stove. Grandma asked her who she was and what she wanted. The woman did not seem to listen to her. Grandma came close to her and the woman started floating in the air. Grandma was scared. She tried to frighten the woman away with a broom, and the ghost, also scared, went through the tiles of the roof and flew, flew away in the night. Grandma says that ghosts always come back. You never know when, but they come.

She then looks at her hand through the white hair and says, "Look, my palms don't have any lines. I lost all of them washing other people's clothes. I would go to the river and scrub clothes all day long. That is how I lost my lines."

Grandma got married to a man who liked to have other women besides her. One day he left and Grandma had to work and raise the children by herself. The only thing she knew how to do was to wash clothes.

She would wash clothes in the river not far from her house. She had to go early in the morning to soap the clothes, put them in the sun to clear the stains, then rinse them. She hung the clothes on the lines and waited until they were dried by the wind. She pressed and folded the clothes. They were clean. Next week they would come back, and she would wash and fold and make them clean again.

Grandma has soft hands and long fingers. Her hands are wrinkled and freckled, but her palms are flat and smooth, like pieces of paper with nothing written on them. She has all these freckles because she got too much sun. She told me that the sun was so strong and bright that she had to work with her eyes almost shut.

"One day with my eyes shut, I wondered: Is he coming back? Why did he leave? Was he not happy? What is going to happen? And then I heard my name: 'Tonica, Tonica, Tonica, the sheet!' I opened my eyes and I could not see anything. It was so bright. Little by little I saw a sheet and a nightgown floating away, far from my reach. Oh my—what am I going to do? Are they coming back? At the shore I was and there I stayed, seeing the sheet and the nightgown going down the river.

"Later that morning when I had almost finished washing the clothes, a little boy, wet and shirtless, came to me with a white sheet in his hands. 'Lady,' he asked, 'Are they yours?' Yes, they were the sheet and the nightgown. He said he was swimming when he saw the clothes floating, and he thought someone might have lost them. I thanked the little boy and pointed to where my house was. I asked him to come in the afternoon. By then I would have a basket of oranges for him."

How Did You Find Me?

Shelly Lovell

ow did you find me?" she asks as I walk through the door to her room. I bend down, kiss her damp forehead. She asks this every time I visit now; I'm used to explaining. Four months since her heart split open one morning like a broken zipper as she rolled from her single bed in the studio apartment downtown on Salmon Street above the newest Starbucks.

They put her in intensive care, six glass rooms in a semicircle around the nurses' station. Monitors and alarms connected her to the nurse on shift. Her hands were tied down with cotton straps, a plastic respirator down her throat. When she was awake, her eyes would roll, she'd toss her head from side to side, and she would cry out indecipherable questions, pleadings. When she was asleep, she was a statue—waxy, yellow, motionless among the tubes and wires that kept her alive.

After 11 days they move her to a regular room. They take the respirator out and my grandmother begins to tell stories. She believes she's been kidnapped by a covert government agency, taken from her family, and held captive. She begs the nurses for scraps of paper, scrawls desperate notes, escape plans, and her children's phone numbers and slips them to strangers during visiting hours. She prays and waits for rescue.

When we arrive to visit, bringing her Almond Joys and Avon lotion, she is so relieved to see us, tears run down her face. Each time we leave she feels herself abandoned and goes back to planning her escape. For a while, she thought she was traveling with Tracy Barry, a local newscaster. She said they'd gone to Paris together and had a wonderful time. My grandmother said she'd enjoyed Tracy's quick sense of humor and the photos of her family she'd brought to share. She thought Tracy's new hairstyle was very flattering.

She is often angry, resentful. She blames us for leaving her in the hospital.

"These nurses are terrible," she tells me "They keep me awake all night long with their parties. They just park me in the hall and play that piano all night. Laughing and carrying on." She shakes her head. "I can't get a minute's rest here. How can you leave me?"

I make her some microwave popcorn, secretly scan the employee break room. I wander the halls, the acrid scent of urine burning my nose. I look the nurses in the eye, read their nametags. I scrutinize them, looking for signs of instability—the sort of recklessness that would allow you to forgo your responsibilities during work hours for a little levity, an occasional sing-along.

I tell her they're always here, checking on you, making sure you're okay. They seem like normal people, more or less, like they care about their jobs. I try to sound convincing. How could they leave you?

She looks away, her blue eyes narrowing. She stares at the muted television.

"You don't know," she says quietly.

One night she complained they'd left her in the hallway next to a man named Ernie who'd tried to touch her breasts. She'd spent the entire night fending him off. Because she just wasn't interested. While the nurses drank and danced and played ragtime on the clandestine piano.

"He was a nice-looking man," she said, "but his teeth were rotten. And besides, I'm too old for all that."

She grew up in a small town in western Pennsylvania. When she was five and her sister two, their mother ran off with a man named Forrest who played piano at the World's Fair. The two girls stayed with Grammy Stewart, not even their real grandmother but a stranger who'd taken in my grandmother's mother as a baby after her own parents said they couldn't afford to keep her.

Our family was rich in a legacy of failed marriages, illicit affairs, and abandoned children.

In the fall, when the garden was fading and the frost was certain to come, they'd pick all the leftover vegetables—the squash and tomatoes, the potatoes and cabbage and pumpkin. They'd put it all in a big cast-iron pot in the backyard on a fire pit. The neighbors would come and bring the end of their gardens too, and they'd make a huge soup for everyone. My grandmother remembered the warmth of fire and the bite of the fall air and playing tag with her friends while the soup boiled. She remembered the bats against the darkening sky and the sound of her family's laughter and the letters from her mother she hoped would soon come.

In August, we move her to a long-term care facility. Her heart has healed but the cancer has returned now and her eyesight is fading. Macular degeneration, they tell us. A camera stuck on its smallest aperture.

We divide up her things. My sister takes the end tables and the flowered couch, my brother the dining table and chairs. Her bed is dismantled and left in my parents' garage. The rest of her furniture is pushed into the third of the room that is hers now.

Mabel and Ester are her roommates, separated by thin metal ceiling tracks with pastel blue hospital curtains. When we come to visit, we don't all fit between the heavy adjustable bed and the dresser with the television. The stuffed teal rocker is pushed against the end of the bed so that when the curtain is pulled, whoever is sitting there is left partly in Mabel's space and partly in my grandmother's.

We gather around the bed. My sister talks in a steady monotonous stream as she files my grandmother's yellowed nails. "Can you believe the dirt in this room," she complains to no one in particular, shaking her head. "You'd think someone could mop the floor now and then. And that smell. . . ."

My mother perches on the edge of the bed, her lips tight, her neck craned to one side in a way that I know will hurt later. She pats the thin covers over my grandmother's legs. My father, in the rocker, his face frozen in a half-smile, holds the curtain to one side to be included in the gathering.

Next door, Mabel clutches her stuffed boy doll, his denim overalls stained, his shirt striped yellow and red, his sewn-on face staring crazily at the perforated ceiling. Mabel whispers to her doll, kisses the side of his cloth face lightly, smiling to herself. She's wearing my grandmother's new pink robe. Some sort of mix-up.

"Jesus Christ," my sister fumes, "I just bought that for her birthday. It's cotton, no lace around the neck—she hates lace—with those exact three buttons. Can't these people get anything right?" I wonder for a moment if she is going to create a scene where we insist that Mabel let go of the doll and give up the robe that rightfully belongs to my grandmother. I picture the nurse's aide, her voice overly loud to compensate for the hard of hearing, her front teeth missing, rolling Mabel over, side to side, as she recovers the robe at my sister's insistence.

Fortunately, we agree, wordlessly, to let this go, too. My mother leaves for the parking lot to smoke. My father takes her place on the side of the bed. We rotate like a well-trained volleyball squad. My sister, in the in-between chair, is silent.

When I was nine and she was between boyfriends, my grandmother shared our three-bedroom apartment. On Friday nights, she'd fix us TV dinners and I'd eat the turkey and stuffing from the foil tray while I'd watch her get ready to go out dancing. She'd put on her false eyelashes and her makeup. She'd iron her dress in her slip and lacquer her blond hair with hair spray out of a big white can. I'd listen to her describe the places she would go and the men she might dance with. I knew she wasn't like other grandmothers. She smoked Pall Malls and went to bars on the weekends. She danced in red dresses. She watched me play jacks on the narrow strip of wooden floor in the dining room, the pink ball bouncing as I filled my hand with the sharp metal pieces. She told me I could be Miss America one day and my talent could be picking up jacks.

On Tuesday I visit at lunchtime. A choir is singing in the day room, the Senior Serenaders, their vests matching baby blue, their cheerful faces flushed in the overheated room. I shut the door of her room but I can still hear their booming rendition of "When the Saints Go Marching In." I sit by my grandmother, holding her hand while she sleeps. When it's time, I feed her the gelatinous turkey and gravy, the boiled corn.

"Mmm," she says, her mouth full of corn. "This is so good." She smiles at me as I wipe her face. Her gown is green and white and dirty from her breakfast.

"Are you the cook here?" she asks, swallowing gratefully.

I tell her no. I tell her I'm her granddaughter.

She nods, smiles again, says my name softly, warmly, as if I'd just entered the room and she was pleased to see me after a long absence.

She walks the hallway between asleep and awake now, always. She nods off midsentence, sleeps a few moments, wakes up crying.

"Why are you crying?"

"It's the end," she says.

"The end of what?"

"Oh you know, the nineteen-something . . . it's very near the end."

Her feet push themselves out from under the sheets and I notice how much they look like my feet. The square toes like small clubs, her legs, her thin calves like mine, resisting muscle. I see myself in her face as she sleeps and I can look at her closely. Her nose is narrow and long; her front teeth protrude more each year. Her hair, always dyed blond and curled high up on her head long after it was in style, is limp now and broken and graying.

The rain comes suddenly after months of sun. The oblong window seems tinted in the late afternoon light. The morphine keeps her at arm's length from everything now, feeds her the dark dreams, her bed a flat boat in a churning sea.

"We were on that thing for so long," she wakes up saying, "and I was cold but couldn't find a blanket. I looked and looked."

She's sweating and I smooth her hair out of her face, her hand in mine.

"I tried to help those children but I couldn't. We were on that thing forever."

Someone's left daisies wilting in a vase above her head on the silent television. She sleeps, wakes again, crying.

"Why are you crying?"

"I think I'm dying, honey, don't you?"

363 Days a Mother

Fern Capella

Today i am a Terrible mother.
fed him sugar for breakfast, mud pies for lunch.
he laps me like horses at a salt lick
with his wide, rough Tongue.
how much ignorance is spoon-fed To our children,
or copied in my shaky movement in our
family life, me a pillar
for his every crumble.
forty lashes for nothing, i strike at him like
a serpent with prey To suck down.
my words burn like acid, bubbling up
his Taffy, sticky sweet skin.
he ate all his Toys, shitting plastic wheels
and resonating like a baby piano,
swaying in chiming Tones of diminishing four
quarter Time, my metronome for chores.
candy for dinner again, i send him To bed,

starving for a blood-filled, beating heart mother.
fall asleep To TanTrums,
pray for my prince.

inTimacy is selling
as a basic human need.
where any woman finds herself,
alone with children, accosted for beauty.
Today i am a Typical mother.
he eats food double fisted, i encourage creativity.
ThoughTs wander over elecTric wires, dangerous Territory.
i reel us in with Tired patience Twice my age.
in alphabet and numeral i can name my child's heroes,
voices To crowd empty galleries of sound with no body around.
we make our circus journey out in public,
preTend we aren'T chaos swimming in Two bodies,
humor a childless society with benT necks, whispered reactions.
he finds a place To open up, express himself emotionally.
i Temper his TanTrum with rigid fingers like god silencing a blizzard,
five-prong rakes curled around The fleshiness of baby Thigh.
There was no righT response, i didn'T give iT,
They glare aT me To change iT.
we run home To our forTress of safety and women, i dig in To
curves on The couch while he digs in To curves on me,
Typical evening aT rest family.

he wakes up, i am babbling and foreign To him.

We dress, eat in silence, brush our hair like licking old wounds, for
Today i am a strange mother.
instantly he disowns me, begs to be better nurtured by a
better woman with a better future.
wetter than goldfish before last bubbles, we stand waiting
for a towel, some-big-body to hold and dry us.
no one comes, i turn to help him out with delayed initiative.
he always forgives.
i am absent, seemingly without child.
he clings, nails in skin, following primal instinct that disgusts me.
we spasm and jerk our way through daily duties,
ritual obligations.
later, he remains insolent at being delivered to his surrogate mother,
though safer than with me, body in and out of earth.
she cuddles and comforts him as the air dissolves around me,
i can't breathe, defer him to her motionless magic,
remove myself to detonate.
retrieval remains resistant, he knows later he will not have me.
we sleep strange in awkward positions, terribly unfamiliar.

we rise simultaneously, growling out hunger,
roll from bed to our clothes.
giggle through breakfast like brothers, swinging knees
for today i am nobody's mother.
i braid hair, do backflips and breakdance,
talk endless about school crushes on toy phones.
he mimics me, my microphone and personal trainer,

rallying behind closed doors.
minus a higher source of power, we struggle less
and sit tepid, motionless, my weakness.
if a man were to find us this way, orphan children
lost and without home, orbiting alone,
he would take pity, but not on me.
i'd be committed and released.
so we dodge bullets in attack mode,
invent crimes, resist as if in crisis
to the nearest threat of dangerous bliss.
Take no prison of attachments, we'll howl
and feed you your own name if you can catch us,
waving blades and hatchets.

Today i am a nihilistic, fatally resistant mother.
in biting terror i find all things overwhelming,
every glimmer in friendly eyes an affront to our faith,
threat to our little territory.
slither from the bed we woke in, sensing snakes and
murderers from the movies running nightly behind eyelids,
still hidden beneath the pillows with the gun.
calling on my chaperones, in the escort of armored cars,
we move through our sequence like movie stars, faded behind
tinted windows, waving in elegantly curled fists, chosen and protected.
with no protection, our day is faint and fragile,
useless against god's chaos

or earth's spin, ridiculed by greek gods of massive strength,
us just barely human.
Today i frighten him, he does not know me shivering,
destructible, and made
of matter, possessing no sure-fire saving grace.
he plays mindless behind darkened shutters, i simmer dinner on low,
stand on armed guard for rapists and child-killers,
cement every door and window.
a woman alone retains defenses,
The child leaves me vulnerable, defenseless.
he nurses to sleep without breathing,
more silent than the stalker haunting our empty
home. i pay deference to space and stars, god and aliens,
whoever decides
fate for us, carried womblike and safe through the night.

Today i am the artist mother, the captivated mother, the tender
mother. Today i am the berating and impatient mother, the aggressive
mother, the working mother, the beautiful mother, the awkward
mother. Today i am the shiva mother, the monster mother, the abusive
mother, the playful mother, the baseball mother, the father
mother. Today i am the shepherded mother, the confused and disconnected
mother, the sexy mother, the virgin mother,
The aging mother, the teenage
mother. Today i am the startled mother, the consumer mother, the torn
mother, the fierce lioness mother, the absorbed and intoxicated
mother. Today i am my own mother, and nobody's daughter.

Yo Mama's Horrorscope:

It's in the Stars!

Aries (March 21–April 19)
You have a pioneering spirit and think most people are losers. Your charge-ahead attitude pisses off everyone you come into contact with. You're totally narcissistic and think your baby looks exactly like you.

Taurus (April 20–May 20)
You have a dogged determination and work like hell. You're nothing but a goddamn communist. People like you because you are affectionate and charming. Then they find out you are a stalker.

Gemini (May 21–June 21)
You are a quick and intelligent thinker. People like you because you are bisexual. You are inclined to expect too much for too little. This means you are cheap.

Cancer (June 22–July 22)
You are an oversensitive wimp and are always putting things off. You are

sympathetic and understanding of other people's problems, which makes you a sucker. This is why you will always be on welfare.

Leo (July 23–August 22)
You consider yourself a born leader. Others think you are an idiot. Most Leos are bullies and drama queens. You are vain and cannot tolerate criticism. Your children learn young that you will never get off your high horse, so they pretend to respect you.

Virgo (August 23–September 22)
You are the logical type and hate disorder. Your shit-picking attitude is sickening to your friends, family, and co-workers. You are obsessive about your children keeping their rooms clean, so they just shove everything under their beds.

Libra (September 23–October 22)
You love harmony and justice. This means you can't handle the real world and are a total basket case. You listen to all sides of an argument, but never form an opinion. Your children blatantly disregard your authority because they know you'll never be able to decide on an appropriate punishment.

Scorpio (October 23–November 21)
You have a wild imagination and often think you are being followed by the FBI or CIA. You're a vigilant mother. Nothing gets by you—even things that don't actually happen. You have minor influence on your friends and they resent you for flaunting your power.

Sagittarius (November 22–December 21)
You are adventurous and will probably end up in a maximum-security

prison. With your children, you are positive and encouraging. This means that they are spoiled brats destined for little minimum-security cells of their own.

Capricorn (December 22–January 19)

You are conservative and afraid of taking risks. When you do get off your butt to try something new, you get so geeked-out you start acting ridiculously aggressive. You are basically chickenshit. You secretly read *Parenting* magazine.

Aquarius (January 20–February 18)

You have an inventive mind and are inclined to be progressive. You lie a great deal. You are forever trying to overthrow the government, but you post your plans on the Internet, so the National Guard always finds out and foils everything.

Pisces (February 19–March 20)

You're quick to reprimand, impatient, and full of advice. All of your children will perfect the eye-roll by the age of three months. You operate on an intuitive level. This means you are totally incapable of dealing with reality.

Contributors

Annaliese Jakimides's work has appeared in publications from Maine to California, including *Beloit Poetry Journal* and *Mothering*. Her essays have been broadcast on public radio. Her essay "Choice" is included in the collection *Room to Grow: Twenty-two Writers Encounter the Pleasures and Paradoxes of Raising Young Children* (St. Martin's). After living for 25 years on a dirt road in northern Maine, she now lives in an apartment in the old Bangor High School. She creates collages and earrings celebrating our real selves. She will always believe, however, that her most extraordinary creations are her three children, all nest-flyers now.

Amie Downey is a writer, mother, daughter, and wife living in North Ferrisburg, Vermont. She has just finished a book of fiction and is currently working on a collection of personal essays around her mother's end-of-life experience with breast cancer. She plans to open an herb shop this year, inspired by her mother's commitment to herbalism and healing. She encourages all women to take care of their reproductive and breast health. She thanks *Hip Mama* for publishing her first works and giving her voice within the context of mothering in poverty. She sends love, strength, and hope for all other mothers who share similar stories.

Ann-Marie Keene is a noncustodial mother of three who lives in Portland, Maine. She uses her creativity to cope with the hard blows in life, expressing herself through writing, comics, photography of adventures, and scads of artwork in a variety of media. The ongoing process—and organization, and showcasing—can be viewed on her website, www.creativespill.com.

Ayun Halliday is the sole staff member of the quarterly zine *The East Village Inky* and the author of *The Big Rumpus: A Mother's Tale from the Trenches* and *No Touch Monkey! And Other Travel Lessons Learned Too Late* (both by Seal Press). She is *Bust* magazine's Mother Superior columnist and also contributes to NPR, *Bitch,* and more anthologies than you can shake a stick at without dangling a participle. She lives in Brooklyn, where she's semi-hard at work on her next book, *Job Hopper: The Checkered Career of a Down-Market Dillettante* (Seal Press), available in March 2005. Visit her website at www.ayunhalliday.com.

Barry Brown is a family-turned-ER doctor who practices in the state of Washington. He lives in Seattle with his wife, Paula Becker, and their children, Hunter, Sawyer, and Lillie.

Bill Donahue lives in Portland, Oregon. With his daughter, Allie, who is 10, he edits *Biff: The Magazine for Kids and Their Parents.* You can email him at biffmagazine@hotmail.com.

Christine Malcolm is mother to three boys and works as a nurse-midwife in a family planning clinic. In her free time she raises sheep and writes about women's health and parenting. Her articles have appeared in the *Journal of Nurse Midwifery* and *Midwifery Today*.

Eve DeBona is an artist and Ariel's mom. She lives in Oaxaca, Mexico, with Ariel's stepdad, John.

Fern Capella is a mother, political activist, spoken word performance artist, and published writer living in lush and tropical Portland, Oregon. She writes, reads, shouts, breathes, battles, breeds, breastfeeds, and bleeds for dissolution of this destructive nation. She is a Mother of Revolution. You can get inside her free of charge at www.ferncapella.com. Bring your rubber gloves and boots.

Geraldo Valério is a writer and illustrator. His writing has been featured in *Spork* and *Knock*. He also has illustrated many children's books. He lives in Portland, Oregon.

Heather Cushman-Dowdee is the creator of *Hathor the Cowgoddess and the Evolution Revolution* (amusing cartoons and insightful/inciteful commentary about home-birthing, breastfeeding on demand, maintaining constant contact, sharing space, unschooling, and saving the world). She currently lives in Los Angeles and is mama to two—no, three!—little radicals, all rattling around in a tiny apartment in a really big city. As an antidote they spend as much time at the beach as they possibly can. Many, many more of her cartoons can be seen at www.hathorthecowgoddess.com.

Ingrid Block is a refugee from the punk scene who has reinvented herself in academia. She is an independent mother who has a marvelous and very practical child to show for it. She frequently has problems with customs agents and the California Highway Patrol, but if you throw a dinner party, she always brings dessert.

Janice Wood came to San Francisco in the early 1970s from New Jersey, worked as a medical technologist in hospitals, then spent six years in Europe (Seville and Paris) teaching English before returning to San Francisco. She currently teaches ESL and biotechnology at City College of San Francisco. Her 12-year-old baseball-player son now has his own bus pass. They garden together at Fort Mason Community Garden.

Julie Bowles is a sexuality educator and life coach working in the San Francisco Bay Area, where she conducts orgasm and female ejaculation workshops as well as individual sessions. She has a master's degree in feminist psychology and is an experienced homeschooler, a renegade housewife, and the mother of four beautiful children. She is currently working on her first book, an adventure into the depths of women's sexuality in our post-punk, post-hippie, and (allegedly) post-feminist era.

June Day is a tall, lanky actress straddling two worlds. She likes to cook and care for her two mice and one daughter, a shy ghost, and itinerant bees. She is currently searching for a new home without ghosts and bees.

Katherine Arnoldi has received an American Library Association Award, two New York Foundation of the Arts Awards (Fiction, Drawing), the DeJur Award, and the TransAtlantic Fiction Award. *The Amazing True Story of a Teenage Single Mom* was a finalist for the Will Eisner Award in the Graphic Novel.

Kathryn Reiss is the author of many award-winning novels for children and young adults. Her most recent is *Sweet Miss Honeywell's Revenge: A Ghost Story* (Harcourt). She lives with her husband and five children in northern California and teaches creative writing at Mills College.

Kathy Briccetti's essays have appeared in many publications and on public radio. She has written a memoir about three generations of adoptions and absent fathers in her family, and is at work on a murder mystery. Evan will enter middle school this year.

Keely Eastley is a Linklater Designated voice teacher who apprenticed with and was trained by Kristin Linklater. She began teaching in 1987 and has been on the faculty of New York University, Circle-in-the-Square, Classic Stage Co., and Shakespeare & Co., where she is a senior faculty member. She currently teaches voice at Emerson College and the Boston Conservatory.

Kimberly Bright is a freelance writer living in the rural American Midwest, where she is trying with occasional success to become a serene earth mother. Her most recent project is a biography of British guitar legend Chris Spedding. Among her fatal weaknesses are American guitars, Italian shoes, coffee, cheap plane tickets, and British accents.

Kristin Rowe-Finkbeiner is the author of *The F-Word: Feminism in Jeopardy* (Seal Press). She lives in the Northwest with her husband, Bill, their children, Connor and Anna, and their dog, Cowboy. A former political director for a statewide political action committee, Kristin currently works as a consultant and researcher in environmental policy and strategy. She writes about public policy, motherhood, health, and new feminism for a variety of national publications, including *Parenting, Bust, Brain, Child;* literary journal, and *Mothering.*

Laura Allen Sandage lives in Davis, California, with her husband and two daughters, ages seven and 12. Her current pursuits include songwriting, performance improv, freewriting, and hospice volunteering.

Leslie Gore is . . . *scheiße!* Bio? Depending on the day, Leslie Gore is a miscellaneous quack snake-oil salesman in the throes of nicotine withdrawal by order of an obscure African diety . . . or the unpaid kitchen slave of one 13-year-old boy who eats more than six horses . . . or the proud single mother of a soon-to-be world famous artist . . . a bodyworker, energy healer, psychic reader, and priestess of Chango . . . and one of the few people currently living in the San Francisco Bay Area who is actually from there.

Lucinda Marshall is an artist, writer, and activist. In 2001, she founded the Feminist Peace Network (www.feministpeacenetwork.org). Since then, her writing has focused on raising awareness about the relationship between patriarchy, militarism, and violence against women. Her work has been published in numerous publications, including *Al-*

terNET, *Awakened Woman, Off Our Backs, Expository,* and *Z* Magazine. Her art can be viewed at www.artmamagallery.com. She lives with her two wonderful clients in Louisville, Kentucky.

Maia Swift, 14, is feeling lazy and loud. She's bored and can't think of a bio right now.

Marcy Sheiner has edited eight anthologies of women's fiction. She has raised a child, now 37, who was born with hydrocephalus, and she regularly writes for the newsletter of the Hydrocephalus Association. Her memoir, *Perfectly Normal,* addresses a mother's experience raising a child with a disability. Find it online at www.iuniverse.com/bookstore.

Maria Doss lives in Olympia, Washington, with husband Richard and kids Esther and Ray, both named for their great-grandparents. Maria is a graduate of the Evergreen State College, where she learned to love the natural world and the ideal of feminist domestic scientist. Maria and family spend most of their time gardening, baking, and listening to '80s music.

Miriam Sagan is the author of more than 20 books, including *Searching for a Mustard Seed: One Young Widow's Unconventional Story* (Quality Words in Print), which expands on "Widows I Have Known." She teaches online for Writers.com and has taught for University of New Mexico, Santa Fe Community College, College of Santa Fe, and UCLA Extension. She lives in Santa Fe with her husband, Richard Feldman, and daughter Isabel. Her website is Santa Fe Poetry Broadside (www.sfpoetry.org).

Nanci Olesen is the producer of MOMbo, a radio resource for moms. Her commentaries have been heard on many public radio stations, and her full-length shows air on Public Radio International (PRI). MOMbo's mission is to "broadcast the everyday truth about motherhood (in order to save the world)." Check it all out at www.mombo.org.

Olivia Edith is an illustrator/textile designer living in the Big Juicy Apple. She migrated from San Francisco, where she graduated with a degree in illustration from the California College of the Arts. Her favorite motto is, "Be scary, not scared. . . ." Check out her work at www.portfolios.com/OliviaDesigns.

Opal Palmer Adisa is a writer who mothers—or maybe a mother who writes. Her books include the award-winning novel *It Begins with Tears* (Heinemann Publishing) and the upcoming *No Regrets*. Find Opal online at www.daughtersofyam.com.

Sara Crangle lives in Cambridge, England, with her two Yukon-born children, now ages nine and five. She and her partner spend their days PhDing and parenting.

Shelly Lovell was born in Washington, DC, and now lives in Portland, Oregon, working at a psychiatric unit. Her poetry has appeared in the *Sonora Review*.

Sin Derella is losing her mind looking for her lost slipper.

Soo Young Lee currently lives in the glorious city of New York with her new husband and seven-year-old son. They love the richness of the city but recently have been looking westward to the mountains of Colorado. She is a part-time professor of creative writing and English, a freelance writer, and a newcomer to Buddhism. Her family consists of a painter husband and a comic book artist son. She finds so much creative energy in the spirit of their new home and family that supports her writing aspirations immensely. The best moments are when she is at her desk typing, her son is drawing at his table, her husband is painting at his easel, and the studio is filled with the busy sounds of self-expression and happy sighs.

Spike Gillespie lives in Austin, Texas, with her son, the amazing Henry Mowgli Gillespie, 13. Gillespie is most recently the author of *Surrender (But Don't Give Yourself Away): Old Cars, Found Hope, and Other Cheap Tricks* (UT Press). Her website is www.spikeg.com.

Susan Ito's work has appeared in *Growing Up Asian American*, *Making More Waves*, the *Bellevue Literary Review*, and other journals and anthologies. She is the coeditor of *A Ghost At Heart's Edge: Stories & Poems of Adoption* (North Atlantic Books). She lives in Oakland, California, with her family, and is at work on a novel.

YanTra BerTelli resides in Seattle, Washington, with her partner Sarah Talbot and their numerous children and pets. Aside from managing her family's abundant food sensitivities and keeping track of various visitation schedules, she writes and publishes once in a while. Yantra's writing regularly appears in *4321*—the zine she publishes with Sarah. She still writes every day and argues with her children to create the space to do it.

About the Editor

Ariel Gore launched *Hip Mama: The Parenting Zine* from her kitchen counter in family student housing at Mills College when she was 23. Her kid is now taller than she is, but Ariel is still practicing the chaos theory of motherhood, fighting the good fight, and pondering the spirituality of coffee. She's the author of three parenting books and the travel memoir *Atlas of the Human Heart*. Get your very own copy of the zine at www.hipmamazine.com.

Illustration Credits

Selected Seal Titles

Whatever, Mom: Hip Mama's Guide to Raising a Teenager by Ariel Gore. $14.95, 1-58005-089-1. *Hip Mama's* back—dispensing wisdom, humor, and common sense to parents who've been dreading the big 1-3 (or counting the days until 1-8).

Beyond One: Growing a Family and Getting a Life by Jennifer Bingham Hull. $14.95, 1-58005-104-9. This wise and humorous book addresses the concerns of parents who are making the leap from one child to two—or more.

The Big Rumpus: A Mother's Tales from the Trenches by Ayun Halliday. $15.95, 1-58005-071-9. Creator of the wildly popular zine *East Village Inky,* Halliday's words and line drawings describe the quirks and everyday travails of a young urban family, warts and all.

Mother Shock: Loving Every (Other) Minute of It by Andrea J. Buchanan. $14.95, 1-58005-082-4. One new mom's refreshing and down-to-earth look at the birth of a mother.

Toddler: Real-life Stories of Those Fickle, Irrational, Urgent, Tiny People We Love edited by Jennifer Margulis. $14.95, 1-58005-093-X. These clever, succinct, and poignant tales capture all the hilarity, magic, and chaos of raising the complex little people we call toddlers.

The Lesbian Parenting Book: A Guide to Creating Families and Raising Children by D. Merilee Clunis, PhD, and G. Dorsey Green, PhD $18.95, 1-58005-090-5. Drawing on real-life experiences of lesbian families and the latest information from family specialists and researchers, the authors cover each stage of parenthood and child development.

Seal Press publishes many books of fiction and nonfiction by women writers. Please visit our website at www.sealpress.com.